SAVITRI

She who won the boon
of life for Satyavan

Shivdutt Sharma

YogiImpressions®

YogiImpressions®

SAVITRI

First published in India in 2017 by

Yogi Impressions LLP

1711, Centre 1, World Trade Centre,

Cuffe Parade, Mumbai 400 005, India.

Website: www.yogiimpressions.com

First Edition: October 2017

Second Reprint: November 2020

Front Cover Illustration: Vijay Ugale

Disclaimer: This is a work of fiction. While it remains true to the main story of Savitri and Satyavan narrated in the Vana Parva of the Mahabharata epic, certain fictional characters have been introduced for interest and dramatic impact. All effort has been taken to represent certain facts as accurately as they have been gathered from various sources. Any oversights or errors are genuinely regretted.

ISBN 978-93-82742-85-2

Printed at: Replika Press Pvt. Ltd.

King Yudhishtra:

'Oh mighty sage, has there ever been any other woman as chaste and exalted, in the history of men, who being dedicated to her husband suffered so much as Draupadi?'

Rishi Markandeya:

'Yes, there was one. Listen O King, how the exalted merit of chaste ladies was completely obtained by a princess named Savitri.'

– Mahabharata, Vana Parva,
Story of Savitri and Satyavan,
Ch. 1.1-3

Prologue

The writ of fate…

Aswapati, king of the prosperous land of Madra, suffers from infertility and therefore, is childless.

Dyumatsena, king of Salwa is blind; as a result of this, he has lost his kingdom and now lives in exile.

Aswapati has a kingdom, but no son.

Dyumatsena has a son, but no kingdom.

Savitri is the daughter born to Aswapati, through a boon granted by Goddess Savitri.

Satyavan is the son of Dyumatsena and, as his name signifies, a speaker of truth.

Ancient India – Map of North-western Kingdoms of Madra and Salwa (7000 BCE-3500 BCE)

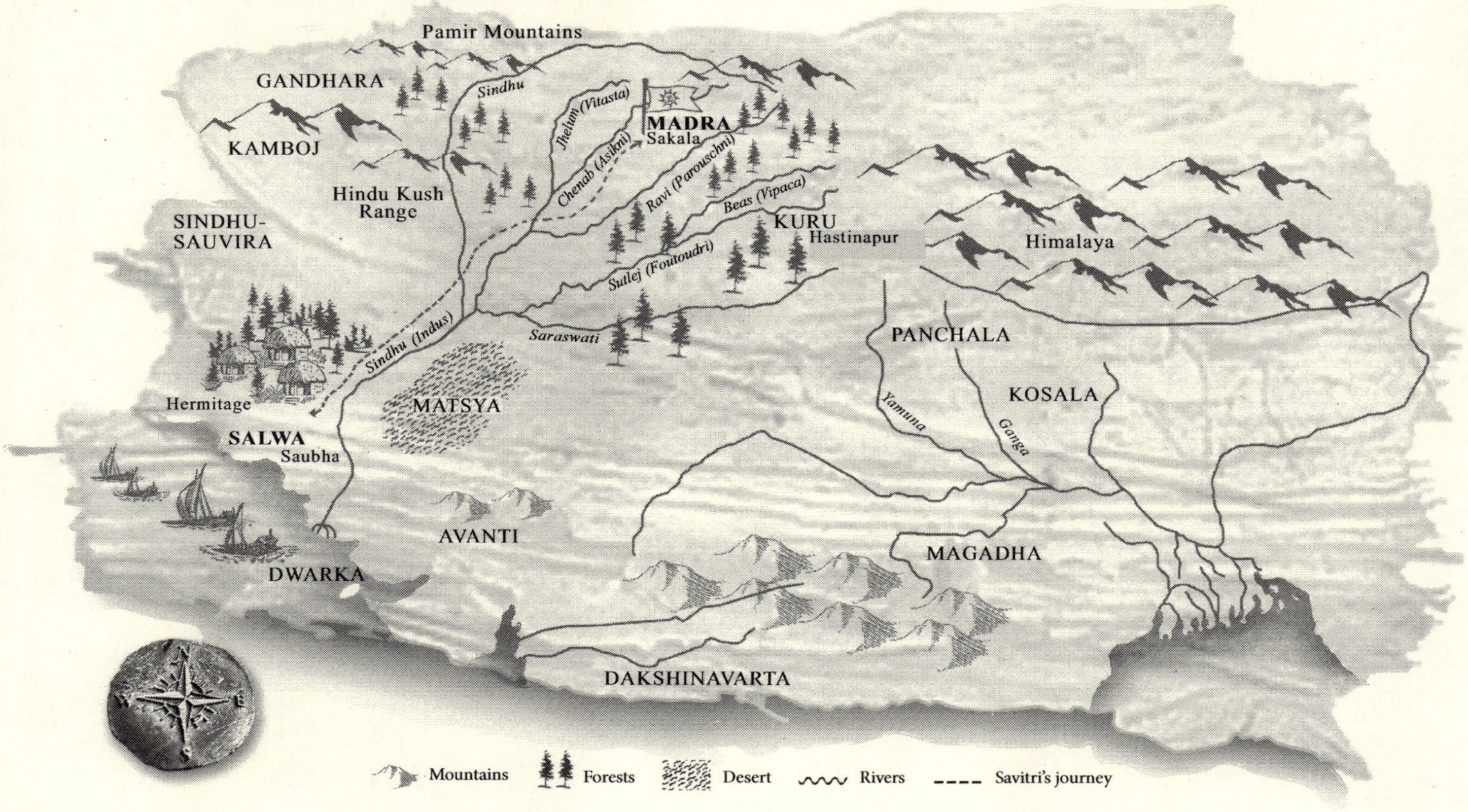

Chapter 1

A Childless King

The rains had come to the kingdom of Uttara Madra, which lay beyond the Pamir mountain range, beyond the Hindu Kush, in a valley between the Chenab and Ravi rivers that flowed through the mountainous landscape. In tiny rivulets they ran nourishing the soil and causing the seeds to swell and sprout in row after row of furrowed land tilled by the farmers. While the earth was being regenerated year after year with showers sent by Lord Varuna from his skies, the gods had not seen fit to favour the pious and noble Aswapati, king of Madra, as kindly.

The palace at Sakala remained bereft of the patter of tiny feet and the laughter of children. His wife, Queen Malavi, the beauteous princess of the Malava clan, had so far not been able to bear a child and provide an heir to the kingdom. Aswapati and Malavi had tried everything, from herbal potions to charmed talismans to magic spells, but nothing had helped. Since even his other wives had been unable to conceive all these years, the King's personal *vaids* and *hakims* were privately led to conclude that the fault lay with the king – he was sterile.

Distressed and distraught, the King withdrew into himself.

One morning as he sat brooding in the lush, green maze of the royal gardens, a deep, rich voice broke his reverie, 'Oh! I've been looking all over for you and here you are… hiding from me, Rajan?'

Looking up, Aswapati's face brightened as he saw the white-robed figure of his *Kul-guru.*

'*Pranam* Gurudev,' he said rising with folded hands and then bending down to touch his feet. 'When did you return from your sojourn in the Himalayas? The ashram has been deprived of your radiant countenance and blessed presence for so long!'

'*Ayushman bhava*, Rajan,' the Guru replied raising his hand to bless the King. 'I trust everything has been going well for you and your people in Madra, during my absence. The kingdom appears to have prospered well. And how is Queen Malavi?'

'Aa-ah here she comes!' he observed. 'You are looking radiant, my child!'

'Pranam Gurudev,' Malavi said and bowed low to touch his feet. Then offering him a glass of milk and a platter of fruits, she added, 'We are so glad to have you back among us.'

'Due to your blessings, which have always been with us, the kingdom is prospering and the people are happy, Gurudev,' said Aswapati.

'Then why do I detect a veil of sadness on your countenance, Rajan?' asked the Kul-guru.

'Wherever I look around me, I see life procreating itself Gurudev. Why then am I accursed to remain childless? This weighs heavily on my mind and I am gravely concerned about the future of my kingdom. There is no heir to carry forward the family line and see to the welfare of the kingdom after I have departed,' said Aswapati resignedly.

'In the course of my *tapasya* and meditations,' said the Kul-guru, 'I have received a message from the gods. You are to perform a *mahayagna* and then go deep into the forests of Madra and perform an eighteen-year long tapasya to the Goddess Savitri.'

'Eighteen years, Gurudev?' exclaimed Aswapati. 'I am already thirty years of age and considered rather old to bear a child. By the time my tapasya is over, I will be fifty years old!'

'The gods work in mysterious ways, Rajan,' answered the Kul-guru. 'Let your faith be steadfast and never let it waver. Everything happens according to the Divine plan.' Saying this, he blessed the King and said, 'Start preparations for the mahayagna to be held ten days from now. I will personally perform it with the help of 108 unmarried youths who are still in the stage of *brahmacharya.*'

'Gurudev, you have observed me since I was a young lad and know I have led a righteous and pious life. I have offered prayers and sacrificial offerings to please the gods. I have been a good ruler of my people and always kept their welfare above mine. Yet, the gods deign to smile on the humblest among them. Why, just the other day, the wife of Kallu who looks after the stables, has been blessed with another male child – her fourth son. And here I am, without a son to even perform my last rites,' lamented Aswapati.

The Kul-guru stroked his flowing beard and said consolingly, 'Rajan, good karma brings its own rewards. And with my powers of divination, I know you have accumulated a storehouse of good karma over your past lives.'

'Then why have not the gods and goddesses thought it fit to bless me with even just one son? I have carried forward my father's name, but who will carry forward mine?' the King said dolefully.

Taking both the King's hands in his, the Kul-guru said, 'There are times the gods test the faith of even those they love, by putting them through agonising ordeals. Just as gold is purified in the goldsmith's fiery furnace of the impure alloys that get embedded in it when it is being mined, so also is this mind-body form through trials and tribulations sent by the gods. These are meant for the evolution of humankind to higher levels of consciousness in each succeeding birth. So do not despair. Give the gods what they ask of you – the eighteen years of tapasya. It will surely yield fruit.'

'Jo aagya Gurudev,' Aswapati said with folded hands.

'Ayushmana bhava,' the Kul-guru reiterated his blessing of a long and fruitful life for the King.

Chapter 2

Praying in the Forest

On the auspicious day declared by the Kul-guru, and with his blessings, King Aswapati cast off his regal robes and donned the saffron *chola* of a monk. Then instructing his chief minister to look after the welfare of the kingdom, he took his leave of Queen Malavi and walked out of the palace towards the dense, dark forest in the foothills of the Pamir mountains.

Away from the hustle and bustle of the kingdom, Aswapati felt a strange relief upon having abdicated the responsibility of his royal duties. He felt free as the eagle flying overhead. A peace and calm began descending upon him as he walked deeper and deeper into the heart of the forest. Even though the sun was now at high noon, the forest was pleasantly cool. The rays of the sun filtering through the trees created a magical play of light and shadows. Aswapati paused to rest and take in his bearings. He would soon have to find shelter for the night because darkness fell much earlier in the forest than it did back in the palace. He took a few *sattu* ladoos from the pouch slung over his shoulder and washed them down with water gulped from his *kamandal*.

Slipping his feet into the flat wooden *khadawa*, he got up and walked towards a hollow opening in a hillock that could be discerned even at this distance. 'That has to be a cave of some sorts,' he mused. 'Perhaps, I can take shelter there for the night.' On reaching the cave, he noticed that someone had spread a mat of dried leaves inside the cave. 'Perhaps a hunter lying in wait for his prey,' he thought. He went out to gather some twigs for building a fire on which he could boil some rice for his supper.

Unused to lying on a reed-thin mat on the stone floor of the cave, he slept fitfully through the night. He woke up at an hour when night began to slowly cast off its cloak of darkness and Surya, in its phase of *Savitr*, began spreading its soft effulgence preceding the dawn of a new day. Picking up his kamandal, he went to bathe in the crystal waters of a stream that he had crossed over last evening. Cupping his palms he scooped some water and then raising them as an offering to Savitr in the heavens, let the water pour back into the stream, while reciting:

"Savitrā prasavena juseta brahma pūrvyam
Tatra yonim krnavase nahi te pūrtam aksipat"[1]

Chanting this mantra, Aswapati took a dip in the stream and then scrubbed his body with the bark of the neem tree. Having thus cleansed himself, he turned his face towards Surya, now rising in the violet sky and offered water to it, intoning:

"Yuje vām brahma pūrvyam namobhir vi śloka etu pathyeva sūreh
Srnvanti viśve amitasya putrā ā ye dhāmāni diviyāni tasthuh"[2]

Today, he was to begin his tapasya as advised by the Kul-guru. The planets and the stars were placed in just the right positions and indicated an auspicious start for the tapasya that would last for eighteen long years in the forest. So, after having bathed he took some clay from the bed of the stream and fashioned an image in the likeness of the female divinity and set it on a platform of stones that he made around the trunk of a banyan tree. Dedicating this rough image in the name of the Goddess Savitri, he placed some flowers before it and offered an invocation to the Goddess:

1 Serve the eternal Brahman with the blessings of the Sun, the cause of the universe. Be absorbed, through Samadhi, in the eternal Brahman. Thus your work will not bind you.

2 O senses and O deities who favour them, through salutations I unite myself with the eternal Brahman, who is your source. Let this prayer sung by me, who follow the right path of the Sun, go forth in all directions. May the sons of the Immortal, who occupy celestial positions, hear it.

- Svetasvatara Upanishad, Ch. 2 – Invocation To Savitr (Sun)

"Om
bhur bhuvah svaha
tat savitur varenyam
bhargo devasya dhimahi
dhiyo yoh nah prachodayat"[3]

Having repeated this mantra 108 times, he sat before the image of the goddess and meditated, soon becoming completely unaware of his surroundings. Over the coming days, Aswapati meditated longer and deeper, completely relinquishing his past concerns and future worries. The past and future, time and space, ceased to exist for him; he became rooted and immersed in the moment. Maybe it was something about the cave, he thought. He had sensed a certain vibration and a palpable occult air about it while he had lain there the first night, so much so that his whole body had tingled with a strange sensation he had never experienced before.

As the days went by his mind gradually stopped turning to his queen, his kingdom and his people; withdrawing deeper into his self. Immune to worldly affairs, his mind stilled. The silence of the forest and the animals inhabiting it became his sole companions. The birds and the beasts soon became reconciled to his presence in their midst. Some, who would earlier watch him warily from a distance, now started approaching closer when he sat cross-legged before the image of the Goddess, offering oblations and reciting mantras and chants in her honour. He had a vague sense that they were also starting to participate in his tapasya as mute spectators.

As weeks drew into months, the tapasya of Aswapati intensified. He experienced his mind becoming blank as a *bhoja patra* on which the gods were inscribing their fresh writ, and felt himself being drawn into their loving embrace.

---

3 Om, Earth Atmosphere Heaven
We meditate on the sacred light
Of the luminous source
May that guide our intentions
[This mantra of Goddess Savitri is also popularly known as the Gayatri mantra.]

Chapter 3

The Blind King

Signs of ill omen had been observed in the skies over the kingdom of Salwa, which lay south-west of Madra, along the Arabian Sea. Political intrigue had been brewing ever since King Dyumatsena's eyesight had begun to fade. When the news reached the ears of an arch rival in a neighbouring kingdom that the King had gone completely blind, he hatched a wily plot to overthrow Dyumatsena and capture the capital city of Saubha.

The chief of a wandering band of *banjaras* on their way to Salwa, was handsomely bribed with a pouch full of gold *mohurs*, to pitch his camp at some distance from the outer walls of the palace and have his most beautiful dancers and musicians entertain the guards on duty. This entertainment was to be provided nightly over a few days to give the dancers and musicians time enough to mingle with the guards, entertain them with wine, women and song to lower their defences. On the dark night of *amavasya*, when the fateful attack was to take place, Chandrakala, along with a bevy of dancers, would serve liquor spiked with a sleep-inducing drug while the musicians would pass around chillums stuffed with ganja and *dhatura* among the guards.

Soon, that ill-fated night arrived and with it came a hand-picked unit of stealthy warriors led by the enemy king. Hooded and clad in black, they moved towards the walls of Dyumatsena's palace where all the guards lay sprawled in a drunken stupor. Throwing ropes with iron hooks at one end over the rampart, they clambered up and opened the gates from within to allow the enemy king and the captain of the armed force into the palace. Using the elements of stealth, silence and surprise, they overpowered everyone and captured King Dyumatsena in what turned out to be a bloodless coup. Along with Saivya, his queen who was still suckling her infant son Satyavan, Dyumatsena was sent into exile in the wilderness on the outer reaches of Salwa.

Here, the blind king and his queen were provided refuge by Rishi Dalbhaya in his hermitage.

Rishi Dalbhaya was a living legend. Tales of his encounter with Parshuram, the sixth incarnation of Lord Vishnu, had been narrated for generations. One such tale stated that when Parshuram was engaged in a battle with King Chandrasen of Ayodhya, his queen Kamala, who was pregnant, escaped from the palace while the battle still raged, and sought refuge in the hermitage of Rishi Dalbhaya. On learning that the Queen had escaped his wrath, Parshuram followed her to the Rishi's hermitage and demanded that he hand over the fugitive Queen to him. Without much ado, Dalbhaya sent for Queen Kamala and presented her to Parshuram.

Amazed at the readiness with which the Rishi had conceded to his demand, Parshuram, in a display of largesse told the Rishi to ask for anything in return. The wise Rishi immediately asked for the life of the Queen's unborn child. Outwitted but bound by his promise, Parshuram agreed to grant Rishi Dalbhaya's wish but with the condition that the boy be brought up not as a Kshatriya warrior, but as a learned scribe and that he should be named *Kayastha*, as he had been saved by his mother's *kaya* – her body.

The wise and compassionate Rishi Dalbhaya, who now lived in the forests of Salwa, was renowned for his knowledge of Ayurveda, of the healing properties of herbs, plants and various barks and leaves of trees. In his hermitage was a grotto dedicated to the worship of Lord Dhanwantri – physician to the gods and goddesses. Dalbhaya had taken it upon himself to tutor the young prince Satyavan from an early age, in the Vedas and the various forms of Yoga, and to impart his wisdom accumulated over years of tapasya and study of the holy scriptures. Occasionally, renowned sages along with their acolytes passing through the forest would stop for a meal or a night's rest at this hermitage before proceeding to their destination in some neighbouring kingdom or pilgrim town.

The name given to a child at birth often shapes and defines his personality. Thus it was only natural for young Satyavan (*satya* = truth, *van* = sayer) to grow up loving the truth. Being the only child, his parents doted upon him and his mother rarely let him wander off too deep into the wilderness when she sent him to collect wood or fetch water. Whenever he had moments to spare, Satyavan could be seen painting scenes from the forest. Although there were no horses to be seen in the wilderness of Salwa, he was often seen moulding horses out of clay or painting them on the walls of his hut, or on large strips of sun-bleached bark. He appeared to be fascinated with them. His mother was puzzled by this fixation on horses and asked Rishi Dalbhaya what it could signify.

'Our young painter, *Chitrasen*, probably has a sub-conscious memory of the horses in the palace of Salwa. The blood of a Kshatriya king runs through his veins and you cannot separate a Kshatriya warrior from his horse,' reasoned the Rishi.

The forest was his world. Satyavan had not known any other. He would listen rather disinterestedly to news of the outside world, which a passing traveller would share with Dyumatsena and his queen. Yet, when his parents were receiving a renowned rishi or sage at the hermitage, he would sit in rapt attention and listen to their discourses on matters pertaining to the physical, mental, as well as spiritual progress of human beings. He would often hear them say, 'Seek out Truth, and you will find God.'

Living in the lap of nature, Satyavan, saw truth in everything he observed around him. The rivers ran true to their course, the birds and animals lived according to their true nature, the shrubs and trees likewise bore their fruit. He instinctively felt and also saw that his mother and father always spoke the truth with each other and with him, never resorting to falsehood. Truth, one could say, had made its home in his heart; truth was second nature to him.

Chapter 4

Raja Yoga of King Aswapati

Three years had passed since Aswapati had donned an ascetic's chola. One day, Queen Malavi sought out the Kul-guru and voiced her concern, 'I wonder how our King is faring in the forest?' she mused. 'Gurudev, perhaps he would welcome a visit from you. Having been his source of strength all along, he may need some advice or further guidance from you.'

Nodding sagely, the Kul-guru said, 'Perhaps you are right. Even I have been wondering how he is progressing in his tapasya.'

'Then it is best if you go to him, Gurudev and, if it is possible, spend a few days with him,' Malavi requested.

'I shall leave on the morrow, Queen Malavi,' assured the Kul-guru.

On reaching the forest next morning, the Kul-guru made his way towards the cave in which Aswapati dwelt. Finding it vacant, instead of going out in search, he thought it wise to just await Aswapati's return. Gathering some twigs and building a fire, he began preparing a broth of wild grain and herbs. He recalled how on his last visit, Aswapati had confessed that he was quite confused about how simply reciting Om, the Savitri mantra and offering oblations to the fire day in, day out for eighteen long years would help him gain the boon he sought

'Rajan, the gods have a specific purpose for this eighteen-year tapasya which they have asked you to perform,' he had replied. 'Consider the first stage to be that of a novitiate who prepares the groundwork with recitation of mantras and chants.'

'And what will come after that?' Aswapati had asked.

'When the time is right, I shall come again and advise you about that. For now, just keep reciting the mantras and chants and sit in meditation,' he had advised.

Now the time had come to prepare the King for the next stage of his spiritual journey.

Seeing him coming from afar, the Kul-guru got up to welcome the King. 'Goodness!' he exclaimed, 'Rajan, how well you are looking! The life of a hermit certainly seems to sit well with you!'

Aswapati smiled, 'Simple living and to an extent, high thinking, Gurudev!'

Said the Kul-guru, 'Hmm... I'm here to prepare you for the next levels of your tapasya. But before that, come sit and have the nourishing broth I have prepared for you.'

While they were enjoying the frugal meal, he began explaining, 'Rajan, although it's true that you have lived a pious and noble life all these years, you were still functioning through the unconscious or subconscious level. The mantras you have been reciting and yagnas you have been performing have enabled you to rise above the mundane level and evolve along the intended spiritual path.

'The Vedic science of consciousness states that there are fourteen planes of consciousness – seven higher planes and seven lower planes – at the sub-human, human and supra-human levels. The Earth, that is physical consciousness, is at the bottom of the higher planes. The planes below it are at our deep subconscious level. To reach the three highest planes – *sat*, *chit* and *ananda* – a human being has to transcend all the planes that are below these.'

'So, performing this lengthy tapasya will help me not only gain access to, but also achieve mastery over these levels of consciousness, and this will finally lead to union with the Divine?' asked Aswapati.

'By doing so, you will connect with the inner 'Self' or the inner 'Divine'. Of course, a lot will depend upon your mental and physical resolve. You will be tested at each plane, Rajan, before you proceed to the next. I hope you follow?' asked the Kul-guru.

'Yes, Gurudev,' Aswapati replied with a smile playing on his lips and requested him to go on.

The Kul-guru began, 'A man is said to be encased in five sheaths of consciousness, known as the *pancha kosas*. The outermost is *Annamaya Purusha* – the physical body of man. Within it, sustaining it and sustained by it is *Pranamaya Purusha* – the vital energy-body of man. Within it is *Manomaya Purusha* – the mind-body associated with man's ego-identity. Within it is *Vijnanamaya Purusha* – this is man's knowledge-body and is associated with wisdom. Within it is *Anandamaya Purusha* – the blissful self. Within these five sheaths is said to live the Eternal Being. By training himself to look inwards and transcending the outer sheaths of consciousness – one can realise the Eternal Being.

'Your tapasya – that is your spiritual journey, Rajan, if pursued with single-minded dedication, will help you reach the pinnacle of your spiritual evolution. Let me forewarn you that it is not going to be easy but, then, nothing truly worth accomplishing comes easily. Traversing through the lower of the fourteen lokas of consciousness could plunge you to the depths of despair and dismay; you will have to struggle and strive hard at every step to attain the next level of consciousness.'

'Gurudev, with your blessings, I shall rise every time I falter along the way,' said Aswapati, undeterred.

'Rajan, more than my blessings, a deeper, fuller understanding of what all this entails will help you most,' said the Kul-guru gently, 'so bear with me and pay heed'.

'There are three *gunas* or qualities of consciousness – *Tamas, Rajas* and *Sattva*. The first is darkness and inertia. The second is inspiration, action and creation. Sattva is knowledge, nobility and sustenance. The fourth, which lies beyond these is, *Trigunaateeta* or the Absolute.

'The states of consciousness in which man perceives the world are the *jagrut* – that is the waking state, *swapna* – the dream state, *sushupti* – the dreamless sleep state and *turiya,* which is the fourth state. In the waking state, the being is called *Vaisvanara* and is outwardly cognitive and perceives gross objects. In the dream state, the being is called *Taijasa,* is inwardly cognitive and perceives subtle objects. In the dreamless sleep state, the being called *Prajna* is blissful, opening up to soul-consciousness. In the fourth *turiya* state, the being is neither inwardly nor outwardly cognitive nor non-cognitive, but it pervades all states of consciousness and none of them. All the other states and all phenomena dissolve in it. It is *Brahman* – the Absolute.'

As he was listening to the sermon with his eyes closed, Aswapati felt a warm ray of light emanating from the brow of his Kul-guru and piercing his own *Ajna chakra,* between his brow. He opened his eyes and looked at his Guru. With folded hands, he bowed low to touch his feet.

'I feel blessed to receive this wisdom from you, Gurudev,' said a humbled Aswapati. 'Whatever the demands this tapasya makes on me, I shall leave no stone unturned in my endeavour to please the goddess Savitri and to receive her blessing and the boon I seek.'

'Rajan, my best wishes are with you. May you be successful in your tapasya and reap the fruits of it,' said the Kul-guru. 'I must take your leave now and return to the palace. Queen Malavi will be most anxious to learn about your welfare and impending return.'

As was his daily practice, Aswapati, having offered ten thousand oblations into the sacrificial fire, followed this ritual with recitations of the Savitri mantra. Thus his yoga tapasya progressed and he kept receiving the rewards of deeper spiritual insights and the power of *siddhis*. This was evident in the visible change that had gradually come over his outward appearance – his face and body resembled that of an enlightened ascetic. His eyes now shone with an inner light. He felt connected to everything around him... he was the leaf stirring in the breeze on the branch of the tree, he was the bird gathering twigs to build a nest, he was the water flowing in the stream, he was the cloud drifting lazily in the sky. He had now begun to identify and experience a unity, a oneness with all things. The transformation that was occurring within him was making every cell in his body open itself to the splendour of this miraculous happening.

The arduous Raja Yoga of Aswapati, that is the Yoga of the King, had first to become Vishwa Yoga of the Universal Being. But even that Yoga had to fulfill itself in the Adya Yoga of the Divine Shakti. Aswapati recognised this and set himself to accomplishing this task because he knew that only then would his tapasya be complete. It is then he would become the Lord of Life; become in truth, the Aswapati. Ashwa, the Horse, a symbol of Life-Energy, the Consciousness-Force in all its power and glory.

It would be this that would lead to the mortal birth of the Goddess Savitri.

Chapter 5

Young Satyavan

One morning Satyavan went along with a group of other young boys from the hermitage to gather herbs and barks for Rishi Dalbhaya. Leading them was Jabala – a rotund, jolly monk who had a large cloth bag that hung over his bulging stomach with its ends tied around his neck. 'Boys,' huffed Jabala, 'I can't walk around with this big bag around my neck. Why don't you go about plucking the herbs while I sit under the shade of this banyan tree?'

'Haha, Jabala! Don't you know that nothing grows under the shade of the banyan?' said Gopala. 'You will remain short and stunted!'

'I am happy as I am, Gopala,' retorted Jabala. 'I don't want to be a tall and gangly lout like you!'

'Stop quarrelling, you two!' Satyavan admonished as he came up to them holding some herbs he had gathered. Putting them into the bag around Jabala's neck, he brushed the mud off his palms. 'Let me tell you something about the forest in which our hermitage stands.'

'What don't we – who have been here longer than you – know about it that you have discovered?' questioned Gopala.

'Oh, shut up Gopala! Let us hear what Satya has to tell us. Anyway, we can do with a break. My fingers are sore from all this plucking and peeling!' said Dhruva.

'Well, it just struck me while we were herb-hunting,' said Satyavan. 'Do you all know that the brave Hanuman once walked this very forest?'

'Oh-ho-ho! That's crazy,' laughed Jabala. 'Have you been listening to the monkeys jabbering in the trees, Satya?'

'It's true, believe me!' said Satya.

'Hmmm...' said one of the group. 'Pray tell us how that could be?'

'It's most interesting, really!' said Satyavan. 'In the *Kishkindha Kanda* of the *Valmiki Ramayana*, it is said that Sugriva, who with the help of Hanuman and Lord Rama, became king of the *Vanaras*, had sent his troops to search for Sita, Lord Rama's wife who had been abducted by Ravana, King of Lanka, in various lands of the Uttarapatha including the kingdoms of Madra and Salwa.'

'That means our lands are really ancient,' replied Jabala.

'Indeed!' said Satyavan. 'They even find mention in the *Vishnu Purana* and the *Matsya Purana*.'

'One must be thankful they did not find Sita Mata anywhere near our lands, else we would have suffered the same fate as Lanka,' Gopala grinned.

'Okay, let's get going now. I still have to collect some dried twigs and branches. Mother needs some firewood for the noon meal. Neither you nor I would want to go hungry, would we?' said Satya.

Rubbing a hand over the generous curve of his stomach, Jabala remarked, 'No, we wouldn't Satya... least of all, me!'

Seeing the boys returning from afar, Satyavan's mother turned to her husband and remarked, 'How well our boy has grown! I wish you could see him now.'

Physical labour had most certainly helped Satyavan develop a lean, sculpted physique. His skin had a healthy, golden sheen to it. The simple, hand-spun clothes made by his mother could not mask the fact that here was a prince among men. He held himself well, with a back straight as an arrow and walked with a measured, princely gait. It was most unfortunate that the boy would probably not inherit his father Dyumatsena's throne, she mused. 'Strange are the ways of our gods and goddesses,'

Saivya thought aloud and shook her head sadly while walking back into her *kutir.*

'There's a time for everything,' she had told him while stroking his hair last night. 'There's a time for sorrow, a time for reflection, a time for adjustment, and a time for action. We have made our peace with your father's blindness. You have now become his second sight and he sees the world through your eyes. Speaking for myself, I have no regrets. I was happy living in the palace, and I am happy living here in this lovely forest. But I know that somewhere deep in his heart, your father feels the loss of his kingship and his kingdom even though he appears to be reconciled to his fate. In fact, I think that being in the company of rishis and sages of the forest has helped him make his peace with the gods for having taken his sight from him. You, of course, were just a babe in arms when we were sent into exile, so you cannot know the depths of his distress at your birthright being snatched away by his enemy.'

'Mother,' he had answered putting his hand over hers. 'I am so happy here. I know of no other world than this sanctuary of peace and calm. And I am not sure I want to either. Let us learn to accept and be content with whatever the gods have provided us.'

Saivya had smiled and continuing to stroke his hair as he had laid his head in her lap, said, 'The gods have provided us with an obedient, dutiful and loving son. What more could we want!'

She had bent her face down to kiss his forehead and observed that he was already fast asleep.

Chapter 6

Aswapati - the Tapasvi

His eyelids fluttered as the veil of night slowly withdrew and the first, faint light at the break of dawn filtered into the cave dwelling. Mild fragrance from the vines of Morning Glory, creeping on the outer wall of his cave, wafted on the light breeze as the violet flowers began to gently unfold their petals. The silent forest gradually came alive with the tweeting and chirping of winged creatures as their chorus of birdsong filled the air.

Aswapati arose and stretching his limbs, stepped out of his cave to go bathe in the icy cold waters of the stream. Winter had just turned to spring; the snows on the mountaintops of the Pamirs had begun to melt and flow down the mountains into the crystal clear streams of the valleys. With the bark of a neem tree, he scrubbed off the ash which he had smeared his body with at night to keep him warm. Washed and bathed, he offered water to the rising sun while reciting a mantra. Then he offered flowers to the Goddess Savitri at her shrine and recited the Savitri mantra. As time had passed, he had found himself naturally getting attuned to the mantra so much so that it was internalised and he kept reciting it sub-consciously during his waking hours. Together with his tapasya, Aswapati had set out to practice and master the various forms of yoga that would help fortify and discipline his mind, body and sense organs to withstand the rigours of advanced yogic practices.

In this deep spiritual retreat, Aswapati gradually lost track of days, then months, and then even years as they came and went. On the rare occasions that his Kul-guru graced him with a visit, he would learn about the welfare of Malavi and the kingdom he had left behind. Two days ago, a herald had been despatched to the forest to inform Aswapati that the Kul-guru would be visiting him today. So to receive him, Aswapati had finished his morning rituals and then gone about gathering fruits and honey to serve the revered sage. Seeing him coming from afar, the King went out to greet him.

'Pranam Gurudev,' Aswapati said with folded palms and then bent down to touch his feet.

'Ayushman bhava... Rajan,' the Guru gave his blessing. 'Queen Malavi sends her regards.'

'How is Malavi taking this long separation from me, Gurudev? How does she occupy her solitary hours?

'Well, Rajan, her tapasya, in a way, is no less ardent than yours. She prays for your well-being and for the success of your severe tapasya. She hopes that the Goddess will be pleased with your devotion and grant the boon that you seek.'

'Come, Gurudev, rest awhile in the cave and let us enjoy nature's fruits. I have picked some fresh wild berries, apples and bananas for you.'

'The forest somehow feels different this time, Rajan,' observed the sage.

'Different in what way, Gurudev? To me, it appears the same as the day I first entered it,' asked Aswapati looking around.

'You have become one with the forest, Rajan, that is why you don't notice it,' smiled the Kul-guru. 'But I feel there is a palpable heartbeat to it. The bark on the trees has a sheen to it, the texture of the leaves looks more silken, the fruits you have picked for me are juicier and glow with the promise of good nourishment – why, even the birds tweet and chirp more sweetly!' he remarked.

Aswapati laughed, 'Gurudev, you see all this because you are in the lap of nature and not in the confines of a man-made, walled city.'

'That's not it, Rajan,' replied the sage sombrely. 'I feel this definitely has something to do with the austere tapasya you have been performing here. What was once a wilderness today appears to be a veritable garden of the gods. The mantras you have been chanting, the yajnas you have been performing in preparation for your eighteen-year sojourn here are making the forest come alive in a most remarkable way!'

'Gurudev, you are a great yogi so your senses are highly refined. It is because of that perhaps that you can see and perceive things that I, still an aspirant, cannot,' Aswapati said in all humility.

'Don't underestimate the powers of your tapasaya, Rajan,' said the sage. 'You are now on the threshold of a joyous discovery – that of your true inner self.'

'With your guidance and blessings, Gurudev, I hope to make good progress.'

'My blessings have always been with you, noble King,' said the sage, giving a gentle smile. 'But remember, a man always reaps the rewards of his own, personal efforts. And I can see that you are sparing no efforts to achieve your goal. Combine that with the power of prayer and you will keep progressing on the path.'

'Yes, Gurudev. But the path appears never-ending,' sighed Aswapti. 'I still have a long way to go.'

'Persevere, pray and persuade the gods. They will surely shower their blessings on you.' Saying this, the sage picked up his kamandal and satchel made of cloth. 'I should be on my way if I am to reach the outskirts of the kingdom before sundown.'

Aswapati stood up. He picked up some fruits from those placed before the image of Goddess Savitri and put them in the Kul-guru's satchel. 'Will you please give these to Malavi as *prasad* from the Goddess, Gurudev?'

'I would be most happy to do so, Rajan. You shall see this prasad bear fruit some day.'

Chapter 7

Divine Visitation

Aswapati awoke feeling a strange lightness of being. The years had passed as if in a dream. And what a glorious dream it had been, he thought as he walked down to the stream. As he stepped into the cold waters, a shiver ran up his spine. His whole body tingled with a strange sensation as he raised his hands to offer water to the rising sun. Its rays seemed to charge the pool of cupped water with golden particles of Divine energy that renewed and invigorated his entire body.

Walking towards the temple-shrine, he picked up a handful of flowers to offer the deity. Pouring water from his kamandal into a dried, curved strip of bark, he washed the feet of the Goddess and decorated her altar with the flowers he had brought. Their fragrance mingled with the scent of freshly-rolled sticks of *dhoop*. He then sat down in the lotus posture and closing his eyes began chanting the *Gayatri* mantra.

As the chanting neared its end, a faint rustling was heard among the leaves that lay spread carpet-like on the forest floor. He sensed a heavenly fragrance spreading throughout the forest. Were his ears ringing or was it the sound of tiny tinkling anklet-bells that seemed to draw nearer? He felt waves of compassion gently coursing through his form and spirit. A strange sense of his space being shared with a Divine presence overpowered him.

Suddenly, Aswapati opened his eyes and saw the forest ablaze with radiant light. Besides the trunk of the tree which housed the shrine, stood the Goddess, a golden aura of light emanating from her form! Almost involuntarily, his arm went up to shield his eyes from her dazzling brilliance.

'O noble and pious King, by the severe austerity, unwavering fidelity and sheer intensity of your tapasya, you have won my admiration for what a mortal being can achieve, when with single-mindedness of purpose he sets out to seek the Divine,' spoke the Goddess. 'This is the moment for which you have waited eighteen years… open your eyes… gaze upon me… and receive my blessing.'

Aswapati unshielded his eyes and gazed upon Goddess Savitri – the Divine Shakti, the daughter of Surya and the consort of Brahma. Overwhelmed and overawed, he found himself at a loss for words, unable to voice his heart's desire.

'Speak not the words… I have heard what is in your heart,' the Goddess said with a gracious smile. 'She will descend possessed of celestial beauty, grace and spiritual power; a heavenly being to be born from a human womb. She will embody the wisdom of the ages, bear an infinite capacity for love, an unshakeable will and an unwavering determination to challenge and overcome the writ of Fate itself.'

'Thus I have been blessed,' murmured Aswapati with folded hands.

'Go in peace, noble King,' said the Goddess, 'Queen Malavi and the kingdom await your return. With the wisdom gained from your Yoga-tapasya, fulfill your kingly obligations and the gods will fulfill theirs.' Then in a flash of blinding light, the Goddess disappeared.

Aswapati bent to pick up the clay image of the Goddess he had worshipped all these years. He touched his forehead to it and returned to the cave he had shared with denizens of the forest who often sought shelter there. He took one last, long look at what had been home to him for eighteen long years and stepped out. As he walked through the forest, the birds and animals that he had befriended accompanied him till the forest gave way to the plains of Madra. Aswapati turned to face them and with folded hands bowed before them.

'My beloved companions, I thank all of you for making my sojourn in your forest so wonderful and enriching. With a heavy heart, I now have to take my leave of you. Your forest is now a sacred sanctuary blessed by the Goddess herself,' said the King. 'My subjects have come to receive me, and the forest awaits your return. I bid you a fond farewell.'

The birds and animals watched the King walk away. Then when he was out of sight, they ambled back to their forest dwelling.

After the welcoming committee of council ministers had greeted the King, Aswapati ascended his chariot and rode towards the palace where Queen Malavi, along with her attendants, was waiting to receive him with fragrant garlands. The people lined along the route, showered petals as the King rode by waving his hand in greeting. The city wore a festive look for their King who was returning to them after such a long time.

Donning the royal robes, Aswapati felt the weight of kingship fall over him once again. After being briefed on the state of affairs in the kingdom and learning that it had continued to prosper under the able governance of his ministers, he declared week-long celebrations and games for the entertainment of his people.

A yagna was conducted at the palace by the Kul-guru to thank the gods for the successful completion of the King's tapasya. Aswapati and Malavi together offered 1008 ladles of ghee to the sacrificial fire as the Gayatri mantra was chanted by them along with 108 brahmachari priests. On completion of the yagna rituals, hymns were chanted in praise of Goddess Savitri.

That night Aswapati visited Malavi in her chambers which had been prepared like a bridal bower, decorated with flowers and lit by myriad bronze and copper lamps whose soft, golden flames flickered and danced. Incense burners cast a bluish haze and veiled musicians behind wooden latticework strummed the strings of their harps to the delicate tinkling of cymbals. Malavi poured a fine *sura* wine from a flagon into a copper chalice and offered it to her husband.

'Dear husband,' she murmured, 'alone and awake I have passed many lonely nights with just the memories of your presence beside me. Tonight we will be one and give form to the blessings of the Goddess.'

As she gently put out the diyas, Aswapati disrobed. When the last flame was gone, moonlight and shadows engulfed the room and the King held his Queen in a tender embrace.

Chapter 8

A Prince among Men

A person's character is shaped by the *samskaras* he consciously or subconsciously receives and imbibes from his parents and grandparents. Samskaras are what define and shape one's, personality and outlook towards others and one's relationship with them.

Satyavan was literally a prince among men. His hair fell in thick and lustrous curls over his strong, square shoulders. His broad, high brow signified the presence of a superior intelligence, while the *tikka* of sandalwood paste that adorned it helped his mind remain focused on the true nature of everything he saw around him. The rishis and sages of the hermitage had given shape to his physical form with various yoga practices that had helped sculpt a perfectly toned and muscled physique. Combined with highly developed meditation techniques, he had also cultivated a healthy mind in a healthy body.

Rishi Dalbhaya saw to the spiritual education of Satyavan. However, there is an essential part of the education of a Kshatriya prince that they could not teach. The commander of the Salwa army, who along with King Dyumatsena had been sent into exile, saw to it that the young prince was trained from an early age in the art of warfare.

'Why do I need to learn the martial arts, Father?' the young prince asked one day. 'I can understand why I must learn the art of the hunt, because we need nourishment for the soul and the body which involves the sacrifice of animals. But we have no enemies in the forest that we will ever have to fight. This is a preserve of peace and harmony that none will venture to disrupt.'

His father, the blind King Dyumatsena, remained silent for a while. Images of his own helplessness and inability to lead the fight against the enemy had risen uninvited to his mind by the boy's question.

'Tell me father, why do I have to learn warfare? I cannot bear the thought of hurting another human being, leave alone killing him in battle,' persisted the youth.

'Son, son... it is the sacred duty of a king to first and foremost protect his people. A king is elected by his tribe because they see in him all the qualities of a leader, provider and saviour. The fact that due to my blindness I failed my people weighs heavily on me. They are now forced to live under the tyrannical rule of my enemy who usurped the throne of your ancestors.'

'But father, you cannot do anything about that now, can you?' answered Satyavan.

At this point, his mother joined in, 'But you can Satyavan. The weight will be on your shoulders to not only uphold but to restore your father – the rightful king – to his throne. You are being prepared for the day when that eventuality arises, and arise it will. At that time, you will have to pick up the sword.'

'Yes mother, by the grace of God I shall see my father on the throne of Salwa, and you by his side,' smiled Satyavan, giving his mother a warm hug.

'O Satya!' shouted Jabala from afar. 'Are you joining us for a swim in the lake?'

'Coming, wait for me!' yelled Satyavan, as he kissed his mother on the cheek and ran off to go with the boys.

'Don't forget your bow and arrow,' called out his mother. 'Bring back a fowl or two for the pot tonight.'

'Yes mother, I will... not to worry,' answered Satyavan as he turned around to wave at her.

Saivya waved back and turned to Dyumatsena.

'Husband,' she said in a voice filled with concern. 'I'm worried that our son is turning into a pacifist in the company of hermits and sages. Although, from time to time, I keep telling him stories about the bravery of our ancestors and about our days when you were the king of Salwa, he barely seems to register the fact that he is a prince in exile and the heir apparent. He seems to think his life will be spent here in the untroubled and peaceful environs of this hermitage in the forest.'

'Saivya,' answered Dyumatsena as he turned towards the sound of her voice, 'let us not forget he is still a mere youth of fourteen years. He has no memories of the palace or of the kingdom we left behind. This hermitage has been the only home he has known. I agree, the company of the rishis and the sages have turned him into a philosopher of sorts – one who by every word and action of his lives the tenet of truth. Falsehood, deceit and treachery are alien to him. In fact, I doubt if he knows anything about that aspect of human nature.'

'I know he has been raised that way, husband,' said Saivya, 'but I also know that someday in the not too distant future, he will have to regain our lost kingdom. We cannot see Satyavan fritter away his birthright to live the rest of his life as a hermit.'

'Well, Saivya, as far as I can see' – and Dyumatsena laughed at the witticism he had unwittingly cracked at his own expense. Saivya hadn't heard him laugh in a long, long time and so, delighted, she laughed along with him.

'So, as I was saying,' he continued once their laughter had subsided, 'as far as I can see – with my mind's eye so to say – our future will be played out as Fate has willed it. You, Satyavan and I – we are just puppets whose strings are in the hands of the gods to manipulate as they will.'

'Fate is one thing, husband,' said Saivya with steely determination in her voice. 'The weakness of human beings lies in attributing the outcome of their lives to Fate. One cannot just sit back and wait for Fate to play out the hand it has dealt us. A person must cultivate and possess the spiritual strength, an unshakeable will power and the courage to challenge Fate. Such a person could even rewrite the writ of Fate and fulfill the destiny he wishes for himself.'

'Now that is an appealing idea, although quaint,' said Dyumatsena with admiration in his voice. 'I can see the influence of Rishi Dalbhaya on your thought processes.'

'Forget about my thought processes, and give some thought to those of Satyavan! He must be made to understand and face the ground reality,' said Saivya firmly.

'Wait for another year or two and he will be ready for marriage. His wife can then nag away at him and bring him down to earth,' laughed Dyumatsena.

'Who will marry a prince in exile?' mused Saivya.

'Is that a rhetorical question?' asked Dyumatsena light-heartedly.

Chapter 9

The Birth of Savitri

She was a child of the breaking dawn. Her birth occurred just when Savitr had dispelled the darkness and tinged the sky above Madra with a rosy hue. The chief midwife sent one of the ladies-in-waiting attending upon the Queen to announce the child's birth to the King.

Aswapati, who had been pacing his chambers ever since he had received word that the Queen had gone into labour, now rushed towards her bedchamber. Bathed and swaddled, the baby lay with her tiny fists and eyes firmly shut next to her mother. However, Malavi's eyes welled with tears as she saw her husband bend over and kiss the baby's forehead.

'Why are you crying Malavi? This is the moment for which we have waited years!' he asked, brushing her tear-stained cheek with his hand.

'Husband,' she sobbed. 'I have borne you a daughter, and not the son you had wished for who would carry forward your name and that of our dynasty.'

'Hush-shh…' he said putting his finger on her lips. 'When the Goddess asked me what I desired, I had asked for many sons to be born unto me. But the Goddess Savitri said that although she had spoken to Lord Brahma about my wish, He had asked her to tell me that soon a daughter of great merit would be born in my house. I had accepted graciously by saying, *'So be it!'* Our daughter, you will see in time to come, will bring great honour and happiness to our family.'

Hearing his words, Malavi smiled, 'Since she is a gift from the Goddess Savitri, then we shall name her Savitri.'

The news that a princess had been born to their King and Queen spread rapidly by word of mouth in the city of Sakala, and in the next few days the royal drummers had carried it across the length and breadth of the kingdom of Madra. As people kept coming and assembling in the palace grounds to offer their good wishes, the royal family came out and presented the newborn to them and graciously received their blessings.

From early childhood, Savitri displayed a happy disposition. A loving child, she was the apple of her parents' eyes and was loved by everyone at the palace. One day while her mother was combing and braiding her hair, the child asked her, 'Mother, I have seen that other children at the palace have brothers or sisters, so why don't I? Even I want a brother or sister I can play with.'

For a moment, Malavi was disconcerted but she regained her composure and said, 'Savitri, you are a special child, a gift of the gods!' hoping that that would not only please her but also satisfy the child's curiosity.

However, Savitri was not to be put off so easily. Like all children, she was naturally curious and persisted: 'But Mother, that doesn't answer my question. Why don't I have a brother or sister? How I wish I had a brother!'

Just then the King entered Malavi's bedchamber. Having overheard the tail-end of the conversation, he patted the child on her head and said, 'I will answer your question, Savitri. Your mother and I tried for many many years to have a child, but we were not lucky. Then our Kul-guru performed a grand yagna. The gods said that if your mother and I wanted a baby, then I would have to perform a strict tapasya for eighteen years in the forest. At the end of my tapasya, Goddess Savitri appeared to me and said that the gods were very happy with my prayers and told me to ask for any boon that I wanted. So, I asked that a very loving, very obedient, very lovely child be born to us. And nine months later, you, my darling daughter, were born.'

'O Father, that is such a wonderful story!' the child clapped her hands delightedly.

'It is not a story my dear Savitri,' answered Aswapati. 'It really happened – just the way I have told you. Ask your mother! Ask our Kul-guru! What's more my dear, you look just like the Goddess – so beautiful, so radiant. You are a very, very special child!'

Savitri looked thoughtful and then said in a soft voice, 'More than I, you are very special parents who stayed apart from each other for so many years, just so I could be born to you. I will never forget the sacrifices you have made and every day from now on, I will pray to the Goddess and thank her for giving me such wonderful parents. I love you both very much. But I still wish I had brothers,' she said, ending wistfully. 'I think I will pray to Goddess Savitri for that!'

The King and Queen laughed at her innocence. 'There will never be a child as special as you are, Savitri. You are all we want,' said her mother. 'Now, go have something to eat before your tutor comes for your morning lessons.'

As the seasons came and went, as the years passed, Savitri grew into a lovely maiden who glowed with an inner divinity and a radiant energy that was visible to everyone who saw her. Her deep knowledge of religion and its oral traditions was largely due to personal tutoring by the Kul-guru. Her grace of form, boundless compassion and natural brilliance were surely a gift of the Goddess herself. Some thought her to be the Goddess Savitri incarnate.

The beauty of the princesses of Madra was legendary and they were the most sought after brides by kings and princes from far and near. The fame of Savitri's beauty – her creamy-white complexion, her lotus-shaped eyes, her winsome smile – had spread even though she was just a young maiden. Offers for her hand in marriage had started arriving early on. But then, Aswapati and Malavi had been loathe to part with their beloved daughter so soon.

On the auspicious day of *parvani,* after bathing at dawn, Savitri went to offer prayers to the gods and goddesses. The presiding priest put flowers and prasad into her hands. As usual, she returned to the palace and went to give the prasad to her father and then touched his feet to receive his blessings.

As Savitri raised herself and her eyes met his, Aswapati was struck by the realisation that his young daughter had now blossomed into a *devrupini*, one as beautiful as a goddess. After she had gone, the King turned to go to the chambers of his chief queen. Seeing the King coming, the Queen's maids-in-waiting covered their faces with veils and informed him that the Queen was in the palace gardens.

Aswapati retraced his steps and went out to the gardens where Malavi, seeing the distressed look on his face, asked what was troubling him.

'Malavi,' the King said, 'have you noticed how our daughter's beauty has ripened with time? We have been blindly ignoring it out of our love for her, but it is time now to think about her marriage.'

'I was wondering when you would open your eyes to that, husband. Whenever I brought up the subject, you always said she's still a child, she's still so young…' Malavi teased.

'I will talk to our Kul-guru about it today itself,' said the King. 'But don't say anything to Savitri just yet.'

Chapter 10

The King's Dilemma

Aswapati was restless. He knew that his mind wouldn't be at peace until he met with the Kul-guru and sought advice on the matter of Savitri's marriage. So he made haste to the Guru's kutir on the palace grounds. On reaching there he found the revered sage sitting under a peepal tree, imparting moral lessons to young acolytes gathered around him. Not wanting to disturb his sermon, he waited under the shade of a tree listening to the sage's perfect enunciation of every word, every syllable. He reflected that apart from the few silver strands in his flowing hair and beard that indicated his Kul-guru was getting on in years, the austerities and asceticism he observed had not seemed to physically age him over all these years. If anything, he looked more robust and imposing.

Seeing the King approach, the Kul-guru wrapped up his sermon and dismissing the class, rose to meet him.

'Rajan, this is your hour of attending to matters of state. Has something happened?'

'No, Gurudev. With your blessings, all goes well with the state of Madra,' said the King. 'I have come to discuss a rather personal matter with you that has been causing me much concern. Malavi suggested that I approach you and take your advice on it.'

'Come, sit down and tell me what is troubling you,' said the Kul-guru putting an arm around Aswapati's shoulder. 'How is Savitri, our angelic daughter? I see she is growing into a very intelligent, confident young woman.'

'Gurudev that is exactly what is of concern to Malavi and me. Just a few years ago, we were continually receiving emissaries from kings and princes seeking her hand in marriage. But of late I have noticed that the proposals are dwindling. That is rather worrying us now. I know we kept dilly-dallying and postponing the matter as we wanted to keep her with us as long as we could. But I fear we were wrong in that,' lamented Aswapati.

'No Rajan, you were neither right nor wrong. It was but natural that both Malavi and you, being blessed with a daughter after remaining childless for so many years, would become attached to her to the point that you could not bear the thought of giving her away in marriage all these years. But God works in mysterious ways...' consoled the Kul-guru.

'Gurudev, do the gods want her to remain unwed?!'

'You of all people should not be mocking the gods, Rajan!' the Kul-guru chided Aswapati. 'I have been observing Savitri. She has grown into a young woman whose beauty, while it beguiles everyone, also has a dazzling brilliance to it. Further, we have spared no effort in her spiritual upbringing. She is also well-versed in all matters of polity and civic affairs. Above all, because she is a heaven-sent child, she radiates a tremendous Divine energy. In fact, she is a *devakanyeti*! And it is these aspects of her persona, although very positive, which are proving to be a hurdle for mere mortals. It has come to my ears that prospective grooms find her rather overwhelming and intimidating. Therefore, they are fighting shy of asking for her hand in marriage.'

'So Gurudev, is it a fault to be perfect?'

'No it isn't, Rajan. But only someone who is the embodiment of perfection himself will be able to complement and accept a living goddess like Savitri.'

'But where on earth will we find such a man, Gurudev?'

'We will not. But Savitri herself will.'

'What do you mean by that, Gurudev?'

'You have heard of the practice of *swayamvara*, Rajan. Let Savitri go forth in her golden chariot driven by the famed stallions of Madra and Kamboja, along with a retinue of our learned sages, diplomats and courtiers. She shall go where her heart leads her, visiting lands distant or near. The gods will be guiding her in her travels. They will surely lead her to such a person who is in the prime of his youth, and knowingly or unknowingly, awaits her coming.'

'So be it, Gurudev. It will be as you say. I will call my advisors and ask them to begin preparations for such a journey,' said Aswapati. 'I will have to confide whatever you have told me to Malavi and I know she has implicit trust in your judgement. As for Savitri, it will be an eye-opener for her, as well as an adventure of sorts to see the world that lies beyond our kingdom of Madra.'

'Trust me, Rajan... we are being guided by the Goddess herself in such a decision,' said the Kul-guru with a confidence that bolstered and overcame whatever reservations the King may have initially had to such a proposal.

That evening while resting in his bedchamber, Aswapati sent for Malavi and told her about the course of action that the Kul-guru had prescribed. Contrary to his expectations, Malavi's face lit up happily as she told her husband that she wholeheartedly agreed with the advice of the sage. As a mother, she told him, she had instinctively felt that this was probably the reason why no one from the royal households of the neighbouring or distant kingdoms had recently come forward lately to ask for the hand of Savitri in marriage. And what better solution was there than for Savitri to go out and choose a husband for herself?

'Rest easy, husband,' Malavi said while running her hand through his hair to soothe and ease away whatever tensions had been brewing in his mind. 'Come, now let us go to sleep. We will talk with Savitri in the morning.'

When Savitri heard what her parents had to say, she was very excited.

'Father,' she said, 'this will be such a wonderful opportunity for me to see what lies beyond our kingdom. I see myself as an ambassador of Madra. You can be assured that I will conduct myself with grace, dignity and decorum at all times.

During these visits, I will also try to establish cordial relations with the kings of the regions that I visit. You know that in your absence, during the eighteen years you were in the forest doing your tapasya, sufficient attention was not paid to such matters. Nothing could have provided a better opportunity than my swayamvara to strengthen our relations. Even those kingdoms that were not very forthcoming earlier will now have no option but to receive us graciously.'

'You are truly wise beyond your years, Savitri. And though you have left it unstated out of deference for me, I know you have realised that the reason you have remained unwed is the fact that your celestial beauty, among all your other qualities, has been posing a deterrent to men who have so far come to seek your hand in marriage,' her father said admiring her acumen. 'And I agree, it does offer us a splendid opportunity politically as well, to establish good relations and trade ties with our neighbours.'

At this juncture, Queen Malavi spoke up, 'All this is well enough, but who will accompany our daughter on her travels? Since she will be gone for months, she will need a retinue of handmaidens and attendants.'

'You don't have to worry Malavi,' said Aswapati. 'I will be deputing some of my senior ministers as advisors, and a unit of handpicked bodyguards to accompany the royal entourage. Forerunners will be despatched to the kingdoms to herald her arrival.'

'When will I be departing, Father?' asked Savitri.

'The Kul-guru is consulting with the astrologers, my dear daughter, to determine the auspicious day when the planets will be placed favourably for such an ambitious venture,' answered her father.

'Let the planets do their work,' said Malavi. 'I will pray to the Goddess Savitri to give me a sign.'

'My patron Goddess!' exclaimed Savitri, clapping her hands in delight. 'I too shall invoke her blessings.'

Chapter 11

Savitri sets out on her Mission

On the auspicious day of *Akshatrittiya*, after having received the blessings of her parents, Savitri rode out of the palace in a chariot drawn by two of the finest steeds from the royal stables of Madra. She was accompanied by the Kul-guru, security guards and her personal attendants. Murmurs of her celestial beauty and the pomp and splendour of the royal train preceded her, even before she entered the cities of kingdoms neighbouring her own.

The eligible princes who came forward to seek her hand were invariably awestruck by her beauty yet, at the same time, felt visibly discomfited by the dynamic energy and brilliant aura emanating from her person. Nor did Savitri come across such a prince, from among the kingdoms to the north, who she felt could be a suitable match. Even the Kul-guru observed that thus far no man worthy of the hand of such a maiden had come forward. In fact what had happened was just the opposite. The kings and princes who had come attracted like moths to a flame had felt their wings singed as they drew nearer, by the almost unbearable radiance of her presence.

Was Savitri, the Kul-guru thought to himself, destined to be admired from afar but remain unpursued, her hand unsought and unclaimed in marriage? Was her inherent divinity, unknown to her, in some way serving as a barrier rather than a blessing towards a matrimonial alliance?

Sensing the unuttered thoughts that were clouding the Kul-guru's mind, Savitri came up to him and said, 'Gurudev, I know what is going on in your mind. You think that perhaps

I am being too fastidious, too demanding by seeking the perfect mate, someone who will stand up to me as an equal in every respect. Yet my heart says he is out there somewhere waiting for me to come to him. I can feel it in every fibre of my being. It's as if his soul is calling out to my soul across the mountains and the plains of this vast land.'

The Kul-guru, recognising the wistful yearning for an idealistic love that would make her feel complete, patted Savitri's shoulder and said, 'Indeed you will find one such, my child. Since our travels have more or less covered the lands of the kingdoms to the north and west of Madra, I think we should now head towards those lying to the south.'

Thanking their hosts for the courtesy extended to them and taking their leave of the last kingdom they had visited, the embassy from Madra left the next morning for the kingdoms towards the south. Travelling through the desert sands of Matsya and keeping close to the bank of the Sindhu river, they would reach the outskirts of the kingdom of Salwa in a few days. Before entering the city, the Kul-guru advised that a scouting party should be sent ahead to see if peace and stability prevailed in the kingdom, or whether it was still beset by unrest. It had been years now since its legitimate ruler, King Dyumatsena, had been sent into exile along with Queen Malavi and their infant son. The scouts returned with the information that Salwa was now under the rule of a tyrannical ruler and his minions who had ruthlessly put down rebellions in the provinces and crushed the spirit of its people.

Since their journey southwards towards Salwa had been long and arduous, the Kul-guru advised that they should rest for a month or two in one of the hermitages of the rishis that dwelt in the forests. Breaking camp, they now headed towards the forests that lay at the base of the mountain range visible in the distance. Winter had just retreated and spring was in the air. Along the tree-line, leaves were starting to uncurl and the earth was renewing itself. The forest dwellers were surprised to see a royal train bearing the flag of Madra, fluttering in the breeze drifting off the coastal route, approaching their sanctuary.

Seeing the ochre-clad, imposing figure of the Kul-guru, some of the forest-dwellers who appeared to be monks and acolytes of some hermitage came forward. Bowing to him, they asked who the travellers wished to meet.

'We come here seeking rest and refuge for a few days,' replied the Kul-guru. 'We will be grateful if you could direct us to a hermitage that would be willing to provide us shelter.'

The monks withdrew a distance and conferred among themselves. Soon, a young monk stepped forward and said, 'We think that the hermitage of Rishi Dalbhaya, which is a little deeper into the forest, would be better equipped to host a royal embassy like yours.' Then turning to a young acolyte, he instructed, 'Balrama, run on ahead and inform our guru, Rishi Dalbhaya, that we have visitors.'

Turning to the Kul-guru, he said, 'Gurudev, I am Prakrit, please come… I shall take you there.'

As they moved deeper and deeper into the forest, the sun's rays pierced the treetops creating a bewitching, dappled play of light and shadow. Savitri felt a rush of goose pimples as she realised they were entering an enchanted place, as the forest appeared to embrace and welcome her in its midst. The trees seemed to bow their heads and sway their branches in the light breeze. Wild hares hopped out of the bushes and into their path, standing frozen for a few moments while their eyes stared at her, before quickly hopping away. The forest came alive with birdsong. A swarm of humming bees froze for an instant in mid-flight and then went buzzing along on their way. A kaleidoscope of colourful butterflies flew towards her and fluttered around her head before flitting away. Savitri instinctively knew that this was the place which destiny had been leading her towards all this time.

An hour later, the visitors arrived at Rishi Dalbhaya's hermitage and were served refreshments by the monks. Everyone was chatting amiably when the sage came out to welcome them with a warm smile.

'On behalf of my monks and myself, I welcome the Kul-guru

of King Aswapati and Princess Savitri to our hermitage,' he said in greeting.

Savitri came forward to touch the sage's feet and while giving her his blessings, Rishi Dalbhaya, intuitively realising that she was no ordinary mortal and was blessed by the gods, welcomed her with the words: 'We are honoured by your presence, Princess. May the purpose of your visit find its fulfillment here.'

'It is I who am honoured to be in your sage presence, Rishi Dalbhaya. My father, King Aswapati, has asked me to convey his respects to you,' Savitri answered with grace and humility. 'Thank you for your blessings Rishi-dev; I do believe my destiny is somehow bound to this place.'

Chapter 12

A Walk in the Woods

The forest awoke at dawn and so did life at the hermitage. The day usually began with prayers to Savitr in the open courtyard lead by Rishi Dalbhaya. On the early morn of this day however, the sage invited the Princess Savitri to lead them into prayer. At breakfast, Savitri expressed a wish to the sage that she be allowed to serve food to the inmates who were all seated on the floor with a green plantain leaf before them. She first served Rishi Dalbhaya, then her Kul-guru and after that, aided by her handmaidens, served the row of monks and acolytes and, lastly, those of her own retinue.

Observing the austere lifestyle of the hermitage, Savitri, keen not to draw too much attention to her royal status, dressed in simple clothes before stepping out for a walk into the forest, accompanied by Sukriti, one her handmaidens. On this fine day, however, she decided to commune with nature and thus, left for her walk unescorted. On her way, she passed by a thatched hut made of bamboos and planks of wood. Sitting outside the hut was a distinguished-looking, middle-aged man who she thought appeared to be blind. As she walked by, she saw a woman come out and serve him a glass of milk. Savitri joined her hands in greeting and walked on.

The white-haired, black-faced baboons chattered away as they swung overhead from branch to branch. Squirrels hopped in and out of holes in the trunks of trees where they had stored their winter ration of acorns. Now, they sat munching on them in patches of sunlight. Savitri waded across a shallow stream that gurgled merrily through the woods. So this is what living in the lap of nature would be like she thought, and was surprised that she found the possibility rather appealing. Coming to a log that lay felled in her path, she felt like resting awhile before exploring the forest any further.

Twirling a lock of hair around her finger, she looked around taking in the sights and sounds of the forest. There is no such thing as utter silence, she mused, at least on this planet. Then another thought struck her. How must that army of ants, climbing in single file on the log she was sitting on, see the world from their viewpoint, or for that matter the serpent that slithered on its belly, or the bird sitting high atop the branch of a tree? Wouldn't their viewpoints be completely different from hers?

'Tuk-tuk…tuk-tuk…' – was that a woodpecker she could hear pecking away on the bark of a tree? If it was, the woodpecker must be quite old she thought, because this was not the rapid 'rat-a-tat' tatting of a younger bird.

She got up, and brushing her garments ventured further into the woods. Plucking a blood-red rhododendron from its branch, she tucked it into her hair just above the ear. The woody scent of pine made her delicate nostrils flare and as she took a deep breath, she felt the chambers of her mind being cleansed and her spirits uplifted. Her senses were sharpened she could tell, because she was aware that now the 'tuk-tuk' sound of the woodpecker seemed nearer. 'But wait, is that really a woodpecker?' she asked herself and paused, head cocked at an angle, and concentrated on the direction the sound was coming from. Was it coming from her left, or from the right? The sound was measured and rhythmic. It paused for sometime and then her ears picked up the sound again. It was much closer now.

A flash of sunlight on metal blinded her for a moment and her hand automatically went up to shield her eyes from its glare. She heard the thud of something heavy hitting the ground. Slowly she removed her hand and blinking her eyes, saw the bare back of a young man who was slithering down a tree.

Unaware of her presence, the young man tied the branches he had chopped into a bundle using a piece of rope and slung it over his broad shoulder. Then he bent to pick up the axe he had dropped earlier and started walking away.

'Listen... listen young man!' Savitri called out to him.

He turned to look back and saw a young maiden walking towards him.

'I have lost my way in these woods. Can you direct me back to the hermitage of Rishi Dalbhaya?'

Their eyes met. He lowered his first. She could not take her eyes off him. His arms and chest were a burnished gold glistening with a film of perspiration from felling wood. A well-muscled torso tapered down towards a slim waist and sturdy legs that swelled at the thighs and narrowed down to taut calves.

He hesitantly raised his eyes noticing first the anklets on her feet, then his gaze moved upward along the fine drape of muslin fabric that clung loosely to her shapely figure, to her waist adorned by a *kamarband* of gold studded with precious gems. Strings of lustrous pearls hung around her graceful, swan-like neck and nestled between her full, rounded bosom that heaved enticingly with every breath she took. The rhododendron tucked in raven-black tresses complemented a divinely beautiful face. The heady fragrance of sandalwood that wafted off her body almost made him swoon.

When his eyes locked into hers, something like an instant spark of recognition – a déjà vu – seemed to pass between them. At that moment, *Kama deva* shot his arrows of love. Making sure they had found their mark, the winged god flew away smiling at his good deed for the day.

Savitri's heart was fluttering like a bird in a cage; her face was flushed. 'I-I... I have lost my way,' she repeated, more flustered than she had ever been.

The youth raised an arched eyebrow and smiled. Savitri felt the warmth of his dazzling smile wash over her in wave upon wave of a heightened sensuousness.

'You should not have ventured unarmed so deep into the forest. One never knows when you might come across a wild animal in these parts. Come, follow me. I am also going back to the hermitage.'

'Do you also stay at the hermitage?' she asked, a flicker of hope in her voice.

'Well, you can almost say that I have been born and brought up in the hermitage, thanks to the kindness of Rishi Dalbhaya,' he answered, as they walked towards the hermitage. 'I live here with my father and mother. And what are you doing in this wilderness? Have you come to meet with the honoured Rishi?'

'Well, not quite… we have been travelling for some months now and needed a place to rest, away from the hustle and bustle of towns and cities. Some kind folk we met on the road suggested this hermitage,' Savitri hedged, not wanting to tell him the real purpose of her visit.

She noticed that the young man had taken a shortcut; presently, they arrived at the hermitage.

'Goodbye,' he said. 'Have a pleasant stay.' Before she could express her thanks, he turned left and disappeared around the corner.

That night, Savitri lay awake tossing and turning, wondering what exactly it was about the young man that had touched her innermost core. When at last she dozed off, he came in her dreams carrying logs of wood as a gift.

Chapter 13

Advice and Consent

Next morning when Savitri came to receive the daily benediction from the Kul-guru, he thought there was something special about the sparkle in her eyes and lightness in her step.

'Pranam Gurudev,' she greeted him with a smile that lit up her face. 'Isn't there something wonderful about this forest and this hermitage? Everyone here is so kind and it all appears so serene and peaceful. I feel I could live here forever and ever...'

The Kul-guru smiled indulgently, 'For a princess brought up in the luxury and comfort of the palace, you wouldn't be able to live here for too long my dear. In fact, I really think we shouldn't be imposing too much on the hospitality of Rishi Dalbhaya.'

The Rishi who was coming towards them, overheard this and laughed. 'How can you be imposing on what I consider a gift of the gods! They have all brought us together here for some purpose... perhaps it will be revealed at the appropriate time. And, Gurudev, I would like some words with you whenever you are free,' he said with a smile.

'Whenever you like... I am at your disposal, Rishi Dalbhaya.'

'Then come, let's go to my hut and we shall talk there,' the Rishi invited. Turning to Savitri, he suggested that while the sun was still not very high, she might find it pleasant to take a walk along the riverbank.

The two sages moved towards a large chestnut tree and sat on a mat which an acolyte hurriedly spread out for them.

'Prahlada, bring us two large glasses of milk and some fruit, if you please,' the Rishi requested.

Turning to the Kul-guru, he came straight to the point. 'My friend, I would like to know what exactly is the purpose of your and the princess's visit to this distant hermitage. It surely is not my fame that brings you here,' he said with a smile. 'After all, it couldn't have been a joyride through the desert kingdom of Matsya, and further down towards the capital city of Saubha, which has been in the throes of strife and unrest these many years since its legitimate ruler was banished into exile.'

The Kul-guru let out a long and deep sigh. 'Rishi-raj, I have no intention of hiding anything from you. In fact, I was thinking of coming to seek your for advice. Aswapati, my King, and his Queen Malavi, were facing what appeared to be a hopeless dilemma. His daughter, the princess Savitri, whom you have met, is the result of a boon granted by the Goddess Savitri, on completion of an eighteen-year long, austere tapasya by my pious and noble King. Savitri is of marriageable age. Her beauty, nobility, piety are famed in all the kingdoms of our land. However, the princes of these kingdoms who have so far come to seek her hand have returned without pressing their suit. According to me, there have been two reasons for this. The first one being that none of them could withstand the dynamic energy Savitri radiates; it is almost Divine in nature. Which man would want to marry a goddess in human form, Rishi-dev? The second reason being that Savitri herself has not shown any particular preference or interest in any of the suitors.'

'Hmm… so…' mused Rishi Dalbhaya, stroking his flowing beard.

'So, her father, the King, asked her to adopt the rite of swayamvara sanctioned by our scriptures, and to go forth and choose a husband for herself among the princes of the north-western kingdoms, near and around Madra. Thus far, this swayamvara has produced no results and I am afraid the mission has been a complete failure. King Aswapati is going to be very disappointed when we return to Madra,' the Kul-guru shook his head in despair.

'Swayamvara is a time-honoured ritual which gives our womenfolk the freedom to choose a husband of their liking,' said the Rishi. 'It's not so unlike the rite of *Gandharva* marriage in which two people in love can, without any family members present and with just the gods as their witness, enter into marriage by exchanging garlands and promising to honour their wedding vows.

'Surely, you are familiar with the romantic legend of Shakuntala whose real father, the sage Vishwamitra, was seduced by Menaka – the most beautiful *apsara* of Indra's court – at Indra's behest?' asked Rishi Dalbhaya.

'I remember hearing of it, but can't recall the exact details,' confessed the Kul-guru.

'Well, to tell it briefly, Shakuntala was born of this union, but was disowned by Vishwamitra and deserted by her mother Menaka who returned to Indra's heaven, leaving the newborn babe in a thicket of the forest. Rishi Kanva found her encircled by a flock of Shakunta birds who had gathered to protect the wailing babe. He adopted her and named her Shakuntala.

'Shakuntala grew up to be a beautiful maiden. One day Dushyanta, the son of Ilina and Rathantara, and king of the lands from Gandhara to the Vindhyas and beyond, came hunting in the forest and saw Shakuntala in the company of her friends. They both fell in love at first sight and married in a Gandharva ceremony.'

'Yes Rishi-dev, but I do recall that Shakuntala's was a troubled marriage. Imagine the indignities she had to undergo, when she was forsaken by Dushyanta. Everyone knows that part of the tale only too well,' said the Kul-guru. 'Our Savitri is a child born of a boon from the Goddess Savitri, a fact that is widely known. I feel this is the main reason why princes and kings have shied away from asking her hand in marriage. And, of course, she cannot marry a commoner Rishi-dev, can she?'

Rishi Dalbhaya patted the sage's shoulder, 'Come, come, don't look so downcast. Everything will turn out alright.

The gods haven't sent you and the princess all this way for nothing, I'm sure,' he added consolingly. 'Let's leave it in their hands. Come inside my hut, I have a rare scriptural work I would like to show you.'

Chapter 14

Love Blossoms in the Wilderness

Savitri's footsteps seemed to move with a mind of their own. Instead of taking the walk along the bank of the river as the Rishi had suggested, her steps led her back towards that neck of the woods where she had run into that handsome woodcutter, who despite his station in life looked like an aristocrat. Today there was no sound of 'tuk-tuk' to indicate his whereabouts. Perhaps he hasn't come today – the thought teased her mind. But her heart told her he was nearby. She heard the cooing of wood pigeons and moved towards the sound.

Resting his head on a bundle of logs, Satyavan lay in a shady glen. One arm was thrown across his eyes as his muscled chest heaved gently with every breath he took. She tiptoed closer to where he lay and stood watching while he slept. His eyelids fluttered lightly and a smile played on his lips as if he was in the midst of a pleasant dream.

Savitri gazed at his broad brow, a sign of wisdom and nobility. His face radiated a passion for living. His hair, a burnished copper, framed what was an angelic face. His body was beautifully proportioned – every limb perfectly chiselled and toned. He was truly 'a prince of the forest,' she mused as a smile played on her own lips as well.

Savitri had been told by her mother that while one is asleep, the masks that one wears in the waking life fall away. One's features and body language during sleep reveal the innermost personality, character and the truth of who we really are.

Savitri could not take her gaze off the sleeping youth. She saw pure innocence, unsullied truth, radiating from his being. Perhaps this was the quality she had been seeking all this while in a life partner and now that she had found it – she vowed to wed herself to him.

Her heart fluttered and leapt with joy in her breast. Of all the places she had visited, Savitri had found love in the wilderness.

She ran a finger along her kohl-lined eyes to smear some kohl on her fingertip. Then very gently, so as not to awaken him, she dabbed a dot of kohl on Satyavan's right temple to ward off and protect him from envious, evil eyes. But would he, she thought, see who had put it there or in an absent-minded move merely wipe if off with the back of his hand? On second thought, she decided to leave a more tangible sign that she had been there. Removing a golden bangle from her wrist, she placed it, together with a blood-red rhododendron, on his gently heaving chest. As she turned around to get up and leave, his hand reached out to grasp her wrist. Startled, she looked back to see Satyavan smiling at her.

'Now that you are here, won't you stay awhile?' he said in an inviting tone, his eyes twinkling with silent merriment.

Savitri tried half-heartedly to pry her wrist loose from his grasp. 'How did you know I would come?' she asked in a slightly breathless voice.

'I knew…' he said, now tenderly caressing her hand which he held in his rough, calloused hand. 'I heard the musical jingling of your anklets as you approached. Besides, there are no women besides my mother in the hermitage. And she for sure doesn't wear anklets nor go traipsing around in the forests.'

'And… an-nd…' Savitri stammered, blushing and flustered, 'you also know who I am?' she asked.

'Yes, I asked around the hermitage. You are the princess of Madra, the praises of whose beauty are sung by minstrels in kingdoms far and near.'

'I too asked! You are Prince Satyavan, son of King Dyumatsena.'

'A king only in name... and I have never known what it is to be a prince,' he said with a rueful smile. 'But, I don't mind. I love the simple life of a woodcutter and I like living in this hermitage with seers and sages for company.'

'Yes, I think I would also love the simple life of a hermitage. Here, one's spirit roams free like the birds and the beasts. Palace life can get rather formal, artificial and ultimately claustrophobic,' mused Savitri. 'This is actually the first time I have been permitted to travel around the countryside, chaperoned by our Kul-guru.'

'Haha, I wouldn't know, never having really lived in a palace. But you would find life hard here with no servants to wait on you; no comforts. Don't you think that you would soon get bored living in a hermitage and long for a life of luxury in your palace back home?' remarked Satyavan. 'By the way, are you on some sort of goodwill mission to the neighbouring lands?

'Well, yes... and no, uh, not really...' Savitri hedged, not wanting to reveal the true purpose of her travels. 'And, to answer your earlier question – no, I would never get bored living in the midst of nature and such serenity. And definitely not with such lovely people as I have met in this hermitage,' she ventured.

'Ahhh, are you implying I am not nice... that I am this boorish woodcutter you ran into in the forest? Didn't I very courteously guide you back to the hermitage just the other day?' Satyavan said teasingly.

'Oh! Now you are making fun of me,' Savitri said petulantly. 'I think I will leave this boorish woodcutter to his own devices; I should not have lingered.'

'Come, come! Don't go away; stay here with me a while longer.' Satyavan made bold said, 'Let us get to know each other better. Tell me about Madra; tell me about the lands you have visited. I have only ever seen this forested haven of Rishi Dalbhaya.'

They spoke for hours. She told him about her parents, about her travels, while he spoke about the lost kingdom of Salwa and his growing up years in the company of seers and sages of the forest. It was late afternoon and Savitri suddenly realised she would be missed back at the hermitage.

'My God! The hours have sped by so fast. I really must be getting back to the hermitage. My maids must be wondering if I have gotten lost again in the forest!' Savitri exclaimed, almost in panic. 'We leave for Madra on the morrow and there is so much to do! I really must rush back!'

'Must you, really? Why can't you stay for a few more days? Please stay on,' pleaded Satyavan in a voice filled with emotion.

'Much as I would love to, Prince Satyavan, I really can't. It's been months that I have been away from my parents and I know they must be longing to have me back with them. Plus, there is one more reason to make haste,' she added, a blush slowly creeping on to her cheeks.

'And pray, what is that reason?' asked Satyavan.

'You will get to know soon enough,' she said mysteriously.

'Is that a promise? And how will I come to know about it?'

'It's more than a promise – it's a vow I make to you,' assured Savitri.

'How I wish you never had to go back!' moaned Satyavan.

'Really? Why would you want that?' asked Savitri, this time hoping to get a clearer indication of what was going on in his mind.

'I am falling in love, Savitri. In fact, I think I am already in love with you.'

Her heart was pounding so loudly, she was sure Satyavan could hear it too.

'I'll make this a heaven on earth for you,' he added alluringly.

'Then I will move heaven and earth to be with you,' answered Savitri.

Chapter 15

Return to Madra

Back in the hermitage, while Rishi Dalbhaya was showing him the scriptural barks, it suddenly struck the Kul-guru, who was sipping on a glass of milk, to ask, 'Rishi-dev, I have noticed that a blind man and his wife live with a young man – obviously their son – in a hut on the premises of your hermitage. Who are these people? They seem to have lived here for quite some time.'

'That, my dear friend, is the exiled King Dyumatsena of Salwa who was banished from his kingdom along with his queen Madri and their son Satyavan. A rival king had invaded their kingdom and usurped the throne some twenty years ago. They have been living here ever since,' revealed the Rishi. 'They have no airs about them and have adapted to a life in the forest very well.'

'So the young man is a prince in exile. He is a grown young man, doesn't he want to reclaim his kingdom?' the Kul-guru wondered.

'All in good time, my dear friend, all in good time,' sighed the Rishi. 'Although he is a Kshatriya prince, being brought up in the hermitage in the company of seers and sages has made him a somewhat mild-mannered and spiritual young man. I cannot see what the future holds for him, but this much I know, the wrong that has been done to this royal family will be righted some day. How and when that will happen, I do not know.'

'Hmm, interesting. Sooner rather than later, I hope,' murmured the Kul-guru. Seeing Savitri returning from her walk, he exclaimed, 'Oh, look! Here comes Savitri.'

Savitri walked with a sense of determination towards them. After greeting Rishi Dalbhaya, she turned to the Kul-guru and said, 'Gurudev, with Rishi Maharaj's permission, I think it is now time to take our leave of his hermitage and return to Madra. We should leave as soon as we can. I am longing to see my parents.'

Turning to Rishi Dalbhaya, she folded her hands and bowing her head in gratitude, Savitri thanked him for the warm hospitality offered to them during their stay, 'I go with your blessings Rishi Dalbhaya, but I have a firm conviction that I will be back here soon. This now feels like my true home and I look forward to the day that I return to your hermitage.'

The Rishi touched her head in blessing, 'You will be welcomed with an open heart, Princess Savitri. With your humility, grace and good nature, you have endeared yourself to everyone here.'

'Can we send our heralds today to Madra to inform my father, the King, that we are on our way back, Gurudev?' Savitri asked the Kul-guru.

'Yes,' said the Kul-guru. Rishi Dalbhaya then said, 'I think Savitri is right and from what I can gauge, she has accomplished what she had set out to do. Go with God, go in peace, Princess. The time has come to fulfill your destiny.'

Chapter 16

Obstacle to Love

After days of travel through desert and mountains, the Kul-guru and Savitri arrived at Madra to a rousing welcome by her parents Aswapati and Malavi.

The King came forward to touch the feet of the Kul-guru, 'It's so good to have you back with us safe and sound. These months away from Madra seem to have done both of you a world of good! Savitri is looking quite radiant, I must say.'

'A fortnight's stay in the hermitage of Rishi Dalbhaya in the forests of Salwa, served as just the elixir we needed to revive ourselves after travelling to various neighbouring kingdoms,' said the Kul-guru.

'So Gurudev, was the mission successful?' enquired Aswapati with a hint of anxiety in his voice.

'Rajan, I think that question should best be addressed to Savitri. Just one look at the glow on her face, that has remained undiminished throughout this arduous journey home, reveals she may have something to tell us,' he said with a smile.

'Come, dear daughter,' said Aswapati putting an arm around his beloved Savitri's shoulders. 'Let us all first take some refreshments, and after you have rested awhile, your mother and I shall wait to hear all about your travels.'

'Let us retire to my chambers Savitri,' said Malavi. 'I have missed you so much these past months and I am sure you have much to tell me. But first you must get some sleep.'

After Savitri and her mother left, the Kul-guru briefed the King about their travels and their stay in the kingdom of Salwa, about its rightful king – Dyumatsena – who had been exiled into the wilderness by a usurper, about the oasis of calm that was the hermitage in which they stayed. He also narrated what Rishi Dalbhaya had to say about the blind king and his wife and, above all, of the high praise the Rishi had for their noble son, Prince Satyavan.

That evening Savitri regaled her parents with tales of her travels through the various kingdoms and the diplomatic courtesies exchanged with the kings of the region. 'Your travels have certainly given you many insights about the lands neighbouring ours, Savitri,' her father said. 'But did you accomplish what you set out for?'

Malavi interjected saying, 'What your father wants to know is, did you meet a prince you liked?'

Savitri smiled shyly. 'Yes, I did!' she said, a blush spreading across her cheeks and her eyes twinkling with joy. She then told them how she had met Satyavan, the prince-in-exile of Salwa, in the hermitage of Rishi Dalbhaya and had chosen him to be her husband. 'We are so perfectly matched, mother,' she exclaimed. 'The moment we set our eyes on one another, we knew we had each found our soulmate!'

Aswapati and Malavi were overjoyed to hear this. 'Then we should start the preparations for your marriage immediately!' said her mother, excited. 'Husband, let's consult the court astrologers and ask them for an auspicious date for the marriage to be solemnised.'

However, the path of true love never runs smooth.

While the palace was busy inset symbol making preparations for the upcoming marriage of Savitri, the Divine messenger of the gods, Narad Muni, came visiting.

'Naa-rayan, Naa-rayan,' chanted Narad Muni to the twang of his tanpura which rested along his shoulder.

'It is indeed a great honour to have you visit us Narad Muni, and your timing as always is perfect; you have arrived at the most opportune moment. But first tell us, is all well with the gods in Indralok?' enquired Aswapati.

'Yes indeed it is Rajan; in fact, it is at their behest that I have come here. My visit to *Prithvi lok* was long overdue. But why do you say my visit is most opportune?'

'We have some good news to share with you, Rishi Narad,' the Kul-guru interjected. 'Princess Savitri has chosen a husband for herself, and she has chosen well. We are in the midst of making preparations for the marriage.'

'The gods be praised! Naa-rayan, Naa-rayan! And who, may I ask, is the lucky young man, Rajan?' asked Narad with a twinkle in his eyes.

'He is the young prince Satyavan, son of King Dyumatsena and Queen Saivya of Salwa, who, unfortunately, are now living in exile at a hermitage in the wilderness of Salwa.'

The gleam slowly dimmed in Narad Muni's eyes. 'I see… how did this match come about, Rajan?'

Then turning to the Kul-guru, he whispered, 'How old is Prince Satyavan? Do you by any chance happen to know his date of birth?'

'Yes, Rishi Dalbhaya had casually mentioned it during one of our conversations,' said the Kul-guru in a hushed voice. 'He should be completing twenty-one or so a week from now in this month of *Phalgun*. I had made a mental note of the date of birth, it was either…'

'That's enough information for me, Gurudev,' said Narad in a hushed voice.

Turning to the royal couple, he prodded, 'Yes, so you were telling me how Savitri came across young Satyavan…'

'Narad Muni, we had despaired of finding a suitable match for Savitri for she would never agree to any proposal we put before her,' answered Malavi.

'So Malavi and I, after consulting with the sages, thought that perhaps it would be best to let Savitri choose whom she wanted to marry through the time-honoured rite of swayamvara,' added Aswapati. 'We sent her along with the Kul-guru on a goodwill mission to the courts of various kings of neighbouring kingdoms. Arriving lastly at the kingdom of

Salwa, she met Prince Satyavan, who was living with his parents, King Dyumatsena and Queen Saivya, in the hermitage of Rishi Dalbhaya.'

'Tch-tch... that appears to have been a most unfortunate event, Rajan,' said Narad with a grim face.

'Why do you say that, Narad Muni? The Kul-guru and Rishi Dalbhaya are all praise for the sterling character and qualities of Prince Satyavan!' said Aswapati, taken aback at this pronouncement.

'That may all well be true, but they couldn't have possibly known that which I have just divined. Being a *jnani* and also well-versed in the knowledge of numerology in Sankhya Shastra, I shudder at what I have to tell you,' Narad said with some tremor in his voice.

Malavi paled and felt faint. She grasped her husband's arm for support.

Aswapati squared his shoulders and asked, 'Why, is there something wrong, Narad Muni? What is it that has cast a dark shadow on your countenance?'

'Satyavan is destined to die within a year of his marriage! That is what is wrong, Aswapati! Didn't you even bother to consult astrologers?' Narad spread his hands in despair. 'Do you still want to give Savitri's hand in marriage to Satyavan? Would you want your daughter to become a widow within a year of marriage?'

'Isn't there any solution to this calamitous event, Narad Muni?' asked Malavi.

'Can anyone defy destiny? Can anyone dare confront the Lord of Death, Yama, when he comes to claim a human soul?' asked Narad.

'But there has to some *upaaya* to overcome this obstacle, some pooja that can be performed, or some cows donated to a poor Brahmin... something which might help to remove this *dosha* in Satyavan's horoscopic chart...' pleaded Malavi.

'I am afraid there is nothing you can do, Queen Malavi.'

'So what shall we do now?' asked Aswapati.

'We must persuade Savitri to reconsider her decision, Rajan! Can you ask her to come here? Perhaps she will listen to what I have to say and then maybe better sense will prevail,' suggested Narad.

Looking radiant in the first flush of love, Savitri came and bowed before Narad Muni. 'It is an honour to have you grace our home with your presence, Narad Muni.'

'Come, dear child, sit with us.' Giving her his blessings, Narad said, 'Savitri, I hear you have chosen to wed the young prince of Salwa?'

'Yes, Narad Muni,' replied Savitri happily. 'In him I have seen all the qualities I was looking for in a husband. He is the personification of truth, a loving and obedient son to his parents, completely at peace even while living in exile, and respects all elders like Rishi Dalbhaya and the seers and sages who live in the forest.'

'I fully agree that Satyavan is possessed of all those qualities you have enumerated Savitri, and in other circumstances he would have been the ideal husband for you. But even though he is of noble blood, he is after all a prince in exile, with no hope of getting back his kingdom,' cautioned the sage. 'Do you want to spend the rest of your life living in the wilderness of Salwa? Think, how unhappy your parents would be to see you living in a thatched hut at a hermitage! You must have met other worthy princes in the course of your travels, maybe not as worthy or as handsome as Satyavan, but my advice would be that you choose one of them as your husband... someone with whom your future life and happiness will be comfortable and secure.'

Hearing this, Savitri cringed and shrank back affronted. She turned to face her parents. 'Father, what is this I am hearing! Mother, why is Narad Muni obstructing my marriage to Satyavan? I have observed Satyavan closely during my stay at the hermitage. I have met his parents. If there was anything amiss, wouldn't Rishi Dalbhaya have cautioned me there and then? Is there something I am not aware of?' she pleaded.

Aswapati and Malavi looked at Narad Muni, their eyes silently beseeching him to break the prediction of Satyavan's short lifespan to Savitri gently and tactfully. Narad Muni shook his head sombrely. There was no way out but to put the fact plainly before Savitri.

She saw the look that was exchanged and sounding exasperated, asked, 'Why are you all looking so gloomy? This is a happy occasion. Everyone should be happy for me!'

'Hush, hush, dear child,' Narad said soothingly to calm her down. 'Hear me out, but first calm down and compose yourself. We all agree that Satyavan is not just any prince; he is the best among men. He is all that you say he is. But child, Satyavan is subject to his destiny, as we all are. And destiny has not favoured him with a long life. In fact – and I don't know how to soften this blow – Satyavan is destined to die within the year from the day of his marriage.'

The blood drained from Savitri's face and she paled. 'This cannot be! I am beloved of the gods. They cannot do this to me!' she cried.

'Hush, hush Savitri, the fault lies in his stars, not with the gods. That is why I have come here to advise you to think twice. Choose wisely.'

Hearing this, Aswapati pleaded with his daughter, 'Put the thought of Satyavan out of your mind, Savitri. This one great defect in his horoscope overrides all his virtues of living a life dedicated to the truth, his high sense of honour and duty, and the unwavering devotion to his parents in their hour of need. You have heard the wise Narad Muni say that his days are numbered. Your mother and I would like you to choose another husband for yourself.'

Regaining her composure, Savitri stood straight and looked resolutely into the eyes of Narad Muni, her Kul-guru and her parents, and stated in no unclear words: 'Dear Father, I have already accepted Satyavan as a husband with all my heart, mind and soul. Much as I honour and respect you, I cannot do as you ask. I cannot even think of another. I will either marry Satyavan, or not marry at all!' she said with determination. 'One year of being wedded to him will serve me for seven lifetimes.'

'Beloved Savitri,' cajoled her mother. 'Do not take a decision in haste. Think well over what the sage Narad and your father have to say. Do you realise the enormity of the decision you are taking? Do you even fully understand the consequences of it?'

'Mother, all I know is this: a daughter can only be given away once in marriage, only once can a parent say, *'I give away my daughter's hand in marriage'*, and death can fall but once. These three things can happen only once. In my heart, I am already married to Satyavan and have been given away. With a life short or long, possessed of virtues or bereft of them, once and for all, I have selected my husband. Twice I shall not select.'

Hearing Savitri's plea touched the sage's heart. Turning to Aswapati, he said, 'Rajan, I see that Savitri has made up her mind and she will not waver from her decision. She has committed her heart and soul to Satyavan. I also honour the high moral ground she has taken in saying that once she has chosen someone for a husband, she cannot think of any other. And it is also true that no other person is possessed of those virtues that dwell in Satyavan. Therefore, this union has my approval. You may proceed with the bestowal of your daughter in marriage to Satyavan.'

'Narad Muni, what you say is true and I cannot disobey what you have sanctioned. I shall do what you have said, because you are my preceptor.'

'I am pleased with your decision, noble Aswapati,' Narad said with a benign smile and raising his hand in blessing added, 'May the bestowal of your daughter Savitri be attended with peace! I shall now take your leave, blessed King.'

Having said this, Narad levitated and rose towards heaven.

Chapter 17

The Torment of Malavi

Although a storm raged in Malavi's heart and her mind was in turmoil all through the meeting with Narad Muni, she had wisely held her tongue and kept her own counsel, not wishing to contradict her husband, the King, in the sage's presence.

Later that evening when Aswapati came to her chambers, he found her having a heated argument with Savitri. Seeing her husband walk in, Malavi turned to him in distress.

'This is all your doing, my lord! What kind of a father are you? By the very act of accepting Narad Muni's diktat, you have condemned your daughter to a life of widowhood just a year after her marriage! And this daughter of yours is being as stubborn as a mule. She is adamant that she will either marry Satyavan or else remain a spinster all her life!' Malavi fumed.

'Calm down, Malavi, calm down,' consoled Aswapati. 'I can well understand your torment.'

'What can you understand, husband? What could you understand! You didn't carry her for nine months in your womb! I carried her, tied to the umbilical cord that sustained and nourished her. With your decision, not only have you separated her from this household, you have also made her return to it impossible. What's more, you have condemned her to a life of poverty in some hermitage in a faraway forest. If the prophecy about Satyavan were to come true, which I have no doubt that it will, then she will have to stay with that blind Dyumatsena and his wife, who have no hope whatsoever of regaining their kingdom, considering that the heir apparent will be dead in a year,' lamented Malavi. 'O God! Why me? Why does this have to happen to me?!'

'Mother!' Savitri rose to protest.

'You stay out of this; I am talking to your father!' Malavi said sternly wagging a finger at her.

'Savitri, why don't you go to your chambers, dear.' said her father kindly.

'No father, much as I regret having to disobey you this time, this concerns my whole life and I wish to stay and hear its resolution,' Savitri pleaded.

'Alright,' he said, walking towards a couch. 'Can we all sit down and talk about this rationally?'

'The whole situation is irrational – you with your consent have made it irreversible!' snapped Malavi.

'Malavi, Malavi… listen to me. Hadn't Narad Muni reacted negatively to this union, despite Satyavan possessing every merit and more than can be expected in a young man? Don't you remember him advising Savitri to go and find another husband? Didn't I try to persuade our daughter to change her mind and find another life partner, instead of the one she had chosen? You know we tried our best to dissuade her from this unfortunate marriage,' Aswapati said.

'All is still not lost,' said Malavi. 'Savitri has so far only made her choice known to us. Neither King Dyumatsena nor his queen, nor Satyavan himself knows that he is the one chosen by our daughter. No one will lose face. No promises have been made, so none will be broken or dishonoured. Hasn't it yet sunk into your mind that Narad Muni has said that within a year of marriage, Satyavan will die?'

Torn by anguish, she turned to Savitri, 'Why don't you just get back on to your chariot and go out to choose another young man? Do you even realise what a stigma widowhood is for a woman? Do you think your in-laws won't see you as a curse visited upon them and their son? And, forget us, can you imagine how much worse it will be for you, when they find out that we had known about it all along and yet married you to their son? No, my dear stubborn daughter, of course you haven't!' she railed.

'Mother, you have always told me to follow my heart. You have said the mind is a fickle, meddlesome, mischievous creature but the heart can never be wrong, it always knows what is the right thing to do in any given circumstance. From the depths of my heart, I have accepted Satyavan as my husband. How can I now even think of another? No, not for my next seven births!' Then in a voice filled with conviction she added, 'If faith can move mountains, Mother, then perhaps Fate's writ can also be changed.'

'Savitri, there is a vast difference between the ideal and that which is real. When reality bites, you may rue the decision you have made,' cautioned Malavi. 'As your mother, I only wish the best for you. I also know that once you make up your mind about something, you do not deviate from your decision. But this is a matter of life and death, with repercussions that go well beyond that!'

'Husband,' said Malavi turning to Aswapati. 'Let us call the Kul-guru and hear what he has to say.'

When the Kul-guru arrived, he sensed the palpable tension. Aswapati said, 'We are unable to convince Savitri to change her mind, Gurudev, and Malavi is set against this union.'

'Rajan, there is nothing to be gained by further debating the merits or demerits of Savitri's choice. She has made her decision clear in no uncertain terms. Let us not forget two aspects of the situation we are facing right now: firstly, despite Narad Muni's prophecy, he has finally given his blessings to this union; secondly, I think we are all losing sight of an important fact here. Savitri is no ordinary child. She is a God-given boon to you and Queen Malavi. Also, the young princess is imbued with the spirit and nature of the Goddess Savitri. There has to be some Divine purpose to this situation we find ourselves confronted with. Perhaps some good may finally emerge from it, which for the present remains hidden from us all.'

Hearing the Kul-guru's sage words, Aswapati, and moreso Malavi, were reconciled. Malavi went and hugged Savitri, 'A mother's happiness lies in that of her daughter's. It shall be as you wish.'

Turning to her husband, she said, 'Let us prepare for the wedding.'

Chapter 18

Savitri Returns to the Hermitage

Faced with Savitri's unwavering resolve and combined with the blessings of Narad Muni and the gods who had obviously blessed this union, Aswapati and Malavi began making preparations for Savitri's marriage. While Malavi got busy in getting the wedding trousseau ready for the bride and the bridegroom, Aswapati went into a huddle with the Kul-guru, the Brahmin priests and astrologers of his court to arrive at an auspicious *muhurat* for the wedding.

Malavi sent for the finest jewellers, weavers and embroiderers in the land and asked Savitri to choose whatever she wanted, as well as what she thought would suit Satyavan. Overwhelmed, Savitri swept aside everything that was displayed before her and turning to her mother said, 'But mother, what will I need all this finery and jewellery for in the hermitage? Everyone there wears robes made of coarse cloth. Satyavan himself wears a simple white dhoti and an *angarakha*. Even his parents wear the robes that everyone else wears in the hermitage!'

For a moment, Malavi was flabbergasted and realised the truth of what Savitri was saying. But she soon brightened up and said firmly, 'Savitri, one never knows what turns destiny takes. I have a feeling that things will not always be as hopeless or grim as they are now. When that day comes, perhaps all these will come in good use. So, let's keep them ready. Anyway, you have to dress as a bride for the wedding and for that we need all this finery. Your father and I are surely not going to give you away in a coarse linen robe. You will be decked in full bridal finery befitting the princess of Madra!' Seeing her mother's point of view and pushing dire predictions to the back of her mind, Savitri acquiesced and like any other young bride threw herself excitedly into the wedding preparations.

Runners had been sent out weeks earlier to inform Rishi Dalbhaya of their expected arrival. Came the day when the marriage procession set out for distant Salwa. Once again, Savitri stepped on to the golden chariot. She turned once to look back upon the home she was now leaving for the last time, perhaps never to return. She caught her mother's eye and a look of understanding passed between them. With the crack of the charioteer's whip the horses bounded forward, their galloping hooves raising clouds of dust as they sped through the gates of the palace and towards the outer boundaries of Madra.

After a week, as they neared their destination, Savitri once again gazed upon the austere mountain peaks at whose foothills lay Rishi Dalbhaya's hermitage. Through a leafy green cleft, the bridal entourage now came upon a dirt road that wound its way into the forest. Roused by the sound of galloping hooves and rumbling chariots, a flock of birds arose chirping and twittering, and flew from their perches on the branches of mighty chestnut and deodar trees, flapping their colourful wings. Startled hare and deer jumped in and out of their path. Ahead could be seen the low, thatched roofs of the outlying huts from which rose tendrils of blue smoke curling out of their chimneys.

Malavi glanced at her daughter whose face was flushed pink with excitement and whose eyes held a sparkle. She kept darting looks here and there scanning the inmates who were emerging from the huts and the hermitage.

Smiling indulgently, she said, 'If you spot Satyavan, do point him out to me, Savitri.'

Savitri blushed, 'I think Satyavan must still be out in the forest gathering wood, but out there...' she said, pointing her finger, 'you can see King Dyumatsena sitting outside his hut.'

Arriving at the hermitage, King Aswapati and the Kulguru alighted from their chariot as it came to a halt outside the gates. Rishi Dalbhaya came forward to welcome Aswapati, who respectfully bent to touch the sage's feet. Coming up behind him, Malavi also bowed to the sage.

'Pranam Rishi Muni, I have heard so much about the kindness and gracious hospitality you showered on Savitri; I thank you for it,' she said.

'Ahhh… and where is your lovely child, dear lady?'

'There she comes Rishi Muni; she just stopped to pay her respects to King Dyumatsena and his queen.'

Savitri ran towards the Rishi and bent to touch his feet. Lifting her up with gentle hands, Rishi Dalbhaya, with a twinkle in his eyes, remarked, 'I see you could not stay away too long from our forest abode, Savitri.'

Aswapati tactfully intervened to ask, 'Guruji, you will have divined the purpose of our visit. I would be grateful if you would accompany us to the dwelling of King Dyumatsena.'

'All in good time, Rajan… all in good time,' smiled Rishi Dalbhaya. 'You have travelled a long distance. Come, take some refreshment first and rest awhile.'

An acolyte brought a large copper pot of buttermilk, a pile of flatbreads and a jar of white butter on a clay platter, and served the guests.

Chapter 19

The Proposal of Marriage

Rishi Dalbhaya turned towards the Kul-guru with a gracious smile, 'So, Gurudev, it feels good to have you back with us.'

The Kul-guru laughed softly, 'It is my pleasure to be in your austere company, Rishi-dev.'

'So how do you plan to put your proposal before King Dyumatsena?' enquired Rishi Dalbhaya. 'Seeing the condition the royal family has been reduced to with the loss of their kingdom, they might – considering their constrained circumstances – shy away from this alliance.'

'Rishi Muni, both King Aswapati and Queen Malavi are aware of this circumstance. I would also like to add here that when we returned home to Madra, sage Narad from Indra's court had paid us a visit. The subject of Savitri's matrimonial alliance with Prince Satyavan, whose reputation as an upholder of truth and righteousness has even reached the gods in Indralok, was raised with him,' said the Kul-guru, 'and after much deliberation, Narad Muni had given his approval and blessings to this union saying that this was also the will of the gods.'

The Rishi replied thoughtfully, 'Well, this union that the gods in their wisdom have blessed must be for the greater good.' Then turning to Aswapati he said, 'Come Rajan, let us go meet King Dyumatsena and Queen Saivya.'

'Your Highness,' said the Rishi Muni as they approached Dyumatsena who was sitting under the shade of a Sala tree, 'You have visitors from the kingdom of Madra who wish to meet you.'

Hearing the Rishi's voice, Saivya came out of the hut. 'It is an honour to receive you and your distinguished guests, Rishi Muni. Please be seated while I get some refreshments for everyone.'

'Oh, Your Highness,' said Malavi, 'please don't go to any trouble, we have just eaten at the hermitage. Come, do please sit here with us.'

Touching Dyumatsena's shoulder, Aswapati said, 'King Dyumatsena, I am Aswapati of Madra, and with me are Queen Malavi and our daughter Savitri, whom you have met earlier.'

Dyumatsena smiled at the mention of Savitri, 'Yes indeed, your daughter I have met briefly. She is most gracious and kind, and from what Saivya tells me, also very beautiful. Your fame, Aswapati, has spread far and wide. Who hasn't heard about your eighteen years of tapasya in the forest? But tell me, what brings you so far away from your kingdom to this retreat in the wilderness of Salwa?'

'Your Majesty, I am here to seek a union between your son Prince Satyavan and my daughter Savitri. She has chosen him as her husband through the rite of swayamvara and we have come here to formalise the marriage with your consent and blessings,' answered Aswapati.

'A marriage proposal for Satyavan? Am I hearing right, Saivya?' Dyumatsena turned his blank gaze towards Saivya who was seated next to him.

'Where is Prince Satyavan, Queen Saivya?' asked Malavi. 'I am most eager to see him.'

'He has gone to the forest with some of his friends to collect some herbs I needed. Should I send one of the ashram boys to fetch him?' she asked, directing her question at Dyumatsena and Rishi Dalbhaya.

'He will be returning anytime now, Saivya,' answered her husband.

Turning to Aswapati, he laid a hand on his shoulder. 'My dear Aswapati, why do you want to give the hand of your daughter in marriage to a prince whose blind father, deprived of his kingdom, has been banished to live out his days in exile in this wilderness? Aren't you – forgive me for saying – turning a blind eye to the fact that she will face a life of severe hardship in this forest retreat?'

'Life is not easy in the forest, King Aswapati,' echoed Saivya. 'As you can see, we live the life of ascetics. Savitri will find it very hard, accustomed as she has been to luxury and being waited upon hand and foot, to adjust to and lead a life of deprivation.'

Hearing these arguments, Savitri could not contain herself. 'With your permission, Your Highnesses, and with the permission of my parents, may I be allowed to say something? As I said to my parents, I have chosen Satyavan to be my husband knowing full well the situation he is in now. Once having accepted him with all my heart and soul, I cannot even bear the thought of another. I will not give you, or him, any cause for complaint. I want to dedicate the remainder of my life to caring for both of you, and commit myself to whatever the future holds for Satyavan. My happiness depends on a life lived in the light of truth, of which your son is a shining example.'

Aswapati and Malavi lent their pleas to Savitri's. 'The situation that Fate has placed you and your family in is according to the will of God. And we all must accept God's will. His will has brought Savitri and Satyavan together and He must have a purpose behind it. Then who are we to oppose God's will? Shouldn't all of us instead accept it joyfully?'

Hearing this, the blind king's eyes filled with tears. Clasping Aswapati's hand he said, 'The tales of your tapasya in the forest are still told after all these years in the lands of the northern kingdoms. In fact, you are popularly known as the 'Tapasvi Raja'. And, who hasn't heard of the goddess-like beauty and conduct of your daughter Savitri? In my heart of hearts, I had longed for an alliance with you but, after being deprived of my kingdom, had refrained from pursuing it. What could a king who had lost his kingdom and a prince who had lost his inheritance have to offer for the hand of the princess of as prosperous a kingdom as Madra? Yet here you are, having travelled this far to ask for my son Satyavan in marriage. My heart is gladdened. And since the gods have willed it, Saivya and I would be happy to give our blessings to this union.'

Malavi cleared her throat to speak, 'Forgive me for interrupting, but shouldn't we also hear what Satyavan feels about this marriage?'

Saivya laid a hand on Malavi's shoulder. Smiling at her she said, 'There hasn't been a more obedient, more loving son than Satyavan. As his parents, we know he will happily accept our choice of a wife for him and a daughter-in-law for ourselves.'

While they were talking among themselves, there came the sound of laughter of a group of boys approaching the hermitage. Saivya exclaimed, 'Oh, there comes Satyavan!'

She waved out and went forward to meet him saying, 'Son! Son! Satya… come see who is here: Savitri!'

'What? Mother, how can Savitri be back so soon? You have been teasing me about her ever since she left. This is just too much, Mother!' said Satyavan, half in embarrassment, half in exasperation.

'Son, she has returned with her parents. They arrived this morning just after you had gone to the forest. Come and meet King Aswapati and Queen Malavi, who are most eager to see you.'

'Why me? Why me!' Satyavan sounded flustered.

He saw Savitri approaching and his eyes lit up with joy.

'That is exactly the reason why,' said Malavi giving her son a playful pinch. 'Isn't she the one whom you have been missing around here all these days? You have even taken to uttering her name over and over in your sleep!'

'Oh God, Mother! Shhh, she will hear you…' whispered Satyavan.

Savitri couldn't help but notice the play between mother and son. Seeing her coming, Saivya hurried back to her huband's side.

Smiling broadly at Satyavan, Savitri said, 'See! I have returned as promised.'

'And every day that you have been away, I have notched on strips of bark. In fact, you came in my dream just last night and...'

'Well I am here now. Come meet my parents; they have something to ask you.'

Leading him towards them, she said, 'Father, Mother, meet Satyavan.'

Satyavan came forward and bent to touch their feet.

'Rise Prince Satyavan,' Aswapati said while placing a hand on his head in blessing.

Dyumatsena cleared his throat and said, 'Son, King Aswapati and Queen Malavi have come with the proposal of marriage between you and Savitri. We are all eager to hear from you that...'

Satyavan didn't even let his father complete what he was saying, he simply blurted out: 'Yes, yes.'

Rishi Dalbhaya laughed heartily and everybody present joined in.

'Youngsters are so impatient these days, aren't they Malavi?' said Satyavan's mother happily.

'Indeed, Saivya. In our days no one bothered to ask our consent,' bantered Malavi.

'Oh?' teased Aswapati. 'Do you mean if you had been asked, you would have refused to marry me, Malavi?'

'Oh, hush, not in front of the children, please!' Malavi protested.

'The so-called children will soon be getting married!' Dyumatsena added amid more laughter.

Chapter 20

Savitri marries Satyavan

Aware now of the Divine sanction for this marriage and its significance, Rishi Dalbhaya suggested to the Kul-guru that all the seers and sages dwelling in the forest should be invited to grace the celebrations, so they may also bless the couple on the day of the wedding. He gave instructions to Prakrit, his aide, about the precise location and method of erecting the marriage pandala, and the herbs and condiments that would be required for the *havan kund* in which the sacred fire would be lit.

He then sent for Satyavan's close friends Jabala, Gopala and Shantanu.

'Pranam Rishi Muni,' the boys chorused. 'We are absolutely thrilled to hear about Satyavan's marriage to Princess Savitri.'

'Yes, everyone is happy and looking forward to the ceremony. So boys, I want you to decorate this hermitage with colourful *rangolis*, flowers and vines bearing wild berries and whatever else you can think of to make it look like a fairy tale wedding. Maybe we can put some colourful cloth banners... Oh yes, speak to the Kul-guru of Madra and to Queen Saivya of Salwa and see if we can get the crest insignia of their royal dynasties to display on flags as symbols of this alliance between the two kings.'

A festive air enveloped the hermitage that bustled with activity in the days that followed. Queen Malavi sent gifts of royal robes and jewels through her handmaidens to King Dyumatsena, Saivya and Satyavan. A generous grant of funds was bestowed by Aswapati on the hermitage so that Rishi

Dalbhaya could add to and expand the facilities at his ashram. The days flew by in a flurry of games organised by friends of Satyavan, and feasts organised by the King and Queen of Madra to which everyone was invited.

The day of the marriage ceremony dawned bright and clear. The leaves and fruit of four plantain trees stood at four corners, signifying four directions – east, west, north, south – of the marriage *mandap* which was covered with a canopy of the most beautiful and fragrant flowers of the forest. To the vigorous beat of drums and the sound of flutes and bugles, King Dyumatsena and Queen Saivya, accompanied by Satyavan astride a white mare, along with his friends led the marriage procession to where Savitri waited with her parents and the Kul-guru.

Dressed by her mother in richly embroidered robes and jewels that befitted a princess, Savitri dazzled like an apsara from heaven. After she and Satyavan had exchanged the bridal garlands, they were guided towards the mandap where Rishi Dalbhaya had lit the sacred fire to solemnise the marriage rites.

As the chanting of mantras began and the fragrant scent of ghee and spices that were being ladled and offered to Agni – the fire-god, rose towards the sky, the gods gathered in heaven to join in the celebrations. After taking seven sacred rounds of the sacrificial fire, Savitri and Satyavan first touched the feet of the Gurus and then their respective parents to seek their blessings for a happy married life.

When she bent down to touch Dyumatsena's and Saivya's feet, the King placed his hand, guided by Saivya, on Savitri's head and blessed her saying, *'Akhand Saubhagyawati raho'*.

In the shower of blessings upon the newly married couple, no one noticed King Aswapati drawing off to the side. Visible only to him was Goddess Savitri who had descended from heaven to shower her blessings on the newlyweds. He went forward to welcome her with folded hands.

'It is so gracious of you to honour us with your presence, Goddess Savitri. Bless the newlyweds, so they…'

'I know what is in your heart, Rajan,' smiled the Goddess. 'Do not worry. After all, I am Savitri's godmother; I shall, unknown to her, always be by her side.'

Looking fondly towards the bridal couple, she raised her hand in blessing and vanished in golden rays of light.

The wedding feast in the evening saw almost all the seers and sages of the forest, along with their disciples, gathered at the venue. Mud lamps had been lit along the grounds of the hermitage and paper lanterns hung from the branches of trees swayed in the light breeze. Swarms of glow-worms had landed on bushes and trees. The forest appeared to twinkle and glow with a million lights.

The aroma of a lavish meal, prepared by the cooks and supervised personally by Malavi and Saivya and comprising the cuisines of both Madra and Salwa, mingled with the fragrance of jasmine flowers to whet the appetite. Musicians entertained the guests who were seated in the grounds of the hermitage relishing the grand wedding feast.

The festivities were drawing to an end, when Rishi Dalbhaya clapped his hands for attention. 'I wish to thank all of you for coming and gracing the nuptials of Savitri and Satyavan. The blessings you have showered on them will go a long way in ensuring they lead a happy married life. It is time for all of us to now retire for the evening and give the families some time together,' he said to a round of applause.

Savitri and Satyavan got up from their seat and stood along with their parents with folded hands to accept the thanks of the guests as they filed past the newlyweds to bid them farewell. After everyone had departed, Saivya and Malavi led the newlyweds towards a gaily decorated hut, that had been built for the couple on the instructions of Rishi Dalbhaya, at a distance from other huts and the main hall of the hermitage.

While Saivya poured oil on the threshold before Savitri stepped over it, Malavi had placed a copper vessel filled to the brim with rice across it. Savitri raised her *ghagra* to overturn it and scatter the rice with a gentle touch of her right foot. She then dipped both her palms in a *thaali* containing *alta* and put their imprint on the inner wall of the hut.

Shutting the door behind them, Malavi and Saivya went back to join their husbands at the hermitage.

The silence that had now descended and engulfed the forest was only interrupted by the rhythmic orchestra of chirping crickets. Moonbeams filtered through the leafy canopy of the forest and sneaked their way through the thatched roof of the hut suffusing it with an ethereal glow.

The faint tinkling of her silver anklets sounded as Savitri moved with quickened heartbeats towards the bridal bed that was strewn with colourful petals. A fragrance of wild roses and jasmine intermingled with the heady vapours arising from sandalwood oil that fed the flame in the wrought-iron diya hung from the rafters. Coming up behind her, Satyavan curled his arm around her slender waist and gently seated her on the bed. Hesitantly he stood until Savitri took his hand and drew him down by her side.

'Together at last…' he whispered, his warm breath sensuously tickling her ear and sending her pulse racing.

'Every day apart from you pained my heart. I came as soon as I could… you knew I would come back to you, didn't you?' she said huskily.

'Yes, in my heart of hearts, I knew,' he answered, trailing a finger lightly across her cheek.

She bent her head slightly to remove an earring.

'Here, let me take it off. An immaculate beauty like yours really has no need for such embellishments,' he said in his silky voice.

'And your adornment is the pure light of truth that shines through you,' she answered.

He moved his hand to slide the gold pins that held up her hair and released her raven tresses, which flowed down as she lowered her face to rest on his bare chest.

His nostrils flared as the scent of crushed wild almonds mingled with oil of roses emanated from her flowing tresses, arousing strange yet pleasurable feelings in him. He drew her closer in a loving embrace. As her lips fluttered and brushed his neck, he felt a quickening. It was a night of seemingly endless rapture and supreme bliss, a joyous union of heaven and earth, as two kindred spirits came together and became one.

Chapter 21

The Perfect Wife

Conveying neither by look nor by words their distress at leaving Savitri behind at the hermitage, Aswapati and Malavi took their leave of her the next day with a heavy heart burdened with the foreknowledge of the fate that awaited both her and Satyavan. Then they went to pay their respects to King Dyumatsena and Queen Saivya.

Malavi tearfully hugged Saivya, saying, 'I now leave Savitri in your love and care. I am sure she will be an obedient and dutiful daughter-in-law to you.'

'You don't have to worry, Malavi; be of good cheer,' said Saivya. 'She will be like a daughter to us.'

Aswapati and Malavi then paid their respects and thanks to Rishi Dalbhaya. Touching his feet in reverence to receive his blessings, Aswapati requested the sage to watch over Savitri and be her source of succour and support whenever she so needed it.

'Farewell dear Rajan,' the sage smiled graciously. His eyes took in Queen Malavi and the Kul-guru as he added, 'You have a long journey back to your kingdom. Go in peace; now this is Savitri's home and she will be well looked after by all of us.'

Savitri and Satyavan came to see them off. He saw that she appeared a little forlorn and her eyes were moist now that she was facing the reality of what it meant being separated from loving parents. Squeezing her hand reassuringly, he murmured, 'From now on, we shall give you all their love and more. As for myself, I won't let even a moment of sadness cast its shadow on your lovely brow.'

As Aswapati and Malavi climbed into their chariot, they looked back once and raised their hands in blessing. Savitri and Satyavan stood there until they could see the departing chariot no more.

'Come, shall we turn back now?' Satyavan asked gently. 'I promise I will take you to see them a year from now.'

His words sent a sudden gust of chill through her body. Recovering instantly, she looked up and smiled at him, 'Yes, I will make sure you do!' Clasping each other's hand, they walked back to the hermitage.

Putting all thoughts of a life lived in the lap of luxury and being waited upon hand-and-foot by a bevy of handmaidens behind her, Savitri happily accepted and adapted to the simple life in the hermitage. As soon as her parents had departed and Satyavan had excused himself saying that he had some work with Rishi Dalbhaya, she had gone to her hut. The lingering fragrance of wild roses and jasmine brought a rush of memories of the night spent in Satyavan's warm embrace. A smile kept playing on her lips as she slowly began removing her earrings, rings and bracelets. She unbraided her coiffed hair to let it flow loose and removing her rich, bridal wear, she instead wore a simple shift made of red-dyed cloth. Amazed at the lightness of spirit, and of being, that she felt having divested herself of the heavy robes and ornaments she was accustomed to wearing, Savitri stepped out to pay her respects to Satyavan's parents.

Seeing her coming towards their hut, Saivya who was putting some wet clothes out to dry almost dropped the sheet she was hanging on a rope.

'Savitri!' she exclaimed, surprised. 'What is this you have worn? This simple robe is meant for ascetics who have adapted to the way of life here. You are a newly-wed bride and should dress as one, my dear.'

Bowing to take her mother-in-law's blessings, Savitri smiled and said, 'With all due respect Mother, I have also embraced the life of an ascetic, just as you did when you came to live in this hermitage. This morning, Satyavan also put aside his bridegroom's clothes and has reverted to the simple white dhoti he has been accustomed to wearing. What need do we have of fine clothes and jewellery over here? Simplicity in itself is the most beautiful ornament, as well as adornment, for a woman. Neither gold nor silver ornaments can match the natural beauty of flowers worn in one's hair or around one's neck. I find these simple robes most comfortable.'

Saivya smiled and embraced her warmly. 'Do as your heart wishes, Savitri. Come, would you like to help me with some chores? Then we must collect some vegetables from the small garden I have been tending behind our hut and start preparing a meal. Satyavan should be returning in a while with some firewood.'

As days went by, Savitri endeared herself to Satyavan's parents by the tender, loving care with which she saw to their needs, and by virtue of her gentle manner of speech and graceful conduct at all times. Rishi Dalbhaya, on a visit to their hut one day, remarked to Dyumatsena and Saivya about how well Savitri had adjusted and adapted to life in the hermitage. He also observed that since Savitri's arrival, the forest somehow seemed more verdant and radiant; that a strange feeling of harmony and blessedness seemed to surround everything in and around the hermitage.

'She radiates a powerful, positive energy that is felt by everyone who comes into contact with her,' added the Rishi.

Dyumatsena joined in by adding, 'Even though I cannot see her, I can feel Savitri's presence whenever she is close by and it lifts my spirits.'

Time passed by in a rapturous dream for Savitri and Satyavan. Accustomed to never doing things by halves, she gave her all to this union and revelled in the fulfillment of her love and passion for Satyavan. The pangs of separation she experienced when he was away in the forest grazing the cows, or cutting wood to keep the home fires burning, would turn to unbridled joy at the sight of his return. Satyavan too was equally enchanted and enamoured by Savitri and the couple spent every moment that they could, together. The personifications of truth and beauty, the purity of heart and mind – Savitri and Satyavan lived their days in a state of bliss.

Endowed as she was with a nature of selflessness, Savitri effortlessly took over the running of the household. Whatever time she and Satyavan could spare was devoted to helping Rishi Dalbhaya, who came to rely upon the efficiency of Savitri, in streamlining the management and day-to-day affairs of the hermitage.

In all this, Savitri was not unmindful of her spiritual practice. She awoke at dawn to worship Goddess Savitri and make her offerings to *Mitra*, *Varuna* and *Indra*. Under the guidance of Rishi Dalbhaya who provided ample spiritual nourishment and nurturing, she progressed along her spiritual journey well aware that when the time came for the prophecy of Narad Muni to be fulfilled, it would take all her spiritual strength and resolve to face up to it.

Days turned to weeks and the weeks turned to months…

Chapter 22

The Night of the Dogs

Coming events, it is said, cast their shadows beforehand.

Eleven months had passed when, late one evening as Savitri lay awake beside a sleeping Satyavan, a mournful howling of wild dogs rent the peace of the night. A shudder ran through her body and she quickly went out to drive the animals away before their wailing awoke her husband. Standing at the perimeter of the hermitage, two ferocious dogs snarled and glared malevolently on spotting her; their eyes shining brightly in the dark of the night. Then they slinked away, disappearing into the deep woods. Horrified, Savitri wiped the beads of perspiration that had sprouted on her brow with the corner of her garment, as ripples of fear coursed through her body.

Taking a deep breath, she controlled herself and went back inside. As she lay down beside Satyavan, he rolled over on his side and, still asleep, threw an arm across her bosom and drew her closer him. This habitual, unconscious gesture of his now suddenly took on a different meaning for Savitri – she felt that subconsciously he was seeking her protection. She snuggled closer in his embrace and softly buried her face in the warmth of his chest.

Next morning, the sun shone bright bringing with it the promise of renewing and nurturing life. Shaking off the incident of last night like a bad dream, yet with the foreknowledge of the prophecy now at the top of her mind, Savitri bathed and sat down for meditation. Focusing on a mental image of the Goddess, she felt a deep peace wash over her. After attending to the needs of

Satyavan's parents and having seen him go off with his friends towards the forest, Savitri went to see Rishi Dalbhaya.

As he saw her approaching from a distance, the Rishi observed there was something about the way her shoulders drooped ever so slightly, that indicated Savitri was not her usual bright self this morning.

'Greetings, Rishi-dev,' Savitri folded her hands respectfully.

Giving his blessings, he asked, 'How have you been, Savitri? Why are you looking so pale and drawn – is something disturbing you?' the sage enquired.

Savitri squared her shoulders and attempting a smile, answered, 'It's nothing really, Rishi-dev.'

Deciding not to push his query, he said, 'I have some good news that will cheer you up, Savitri. Your Kul-guru arrived from Madra early this morning.'

Her eyes suddenly lit up. 'Oh, that's wonderful! Are my parents well? Can I go see him?'

'He has gone to freshen up and change his clothes. Sit; he will be joining us shortly,' saying which, the sage turned to one of the acolytes and asked him to bring some refreshments from the kitchen for the guest.

Seeing the Kul-guru coming towards them, Savitri went forward to touch his feet and welcomed him with a cheerful, 'This is such a pleasant surprise, Gurudev! How come…?'

'Your father and mother were anxious to see how you were doing, Savitri. Since I was visiting the kingdom of Surusena on some official work, they asked me to come here and see if I could persuade you and Satyavan to come to Madra for some time,' the Kul-guru replied.

'How are my mother and father, Gurudev? Are they well?'

'Yes Savitri, they are well except for the fact that they miss you very much.'

'So do I, Gurudev, but this is not an opportune time for us to go to Madra. My in-laws would be reluctant to go in their present condition and circumstances, and I would not like to leave them at this time,' Savitri replied.

'I understand, Savitri. But...'

'Gurudev, Savitri, come here and let us sit together awhile,' Rishi Dalbhaya called out to them. 'Your Guruji has had a long journey and he must be hungry. I've already sent Pranjal to bring a bowl of hot porridge for him, and one for you as well as you are looking unusually wan today. Come, have something to eat first and then you can both talk to your hearts' content.'

Having partaken of the morning breakfast, Savitri and the Kul-guru walked towards her hut. Along the way, the Kul-guru enquired after Satyavan and his parents.

'They are well, but Gurudev, I am relieved that you are here. As you know the time is drawing near. We have now been married for eleven months and...' Savitri let the sentence hang.

'That is exactly why your parents have sent me here, Savitri.'

'Gurudev, I have been very disturbed during these past few nights and I don't know how I am going to live through all this,' Savitri broke into sobs.

'Come, come, let's sit down there under that tree. Calm yourself and tell me what happened.'

'Last night, I was woken by the howling of wild dogs – actually, it was more like they were wailing. I went out to shoo them away, afraid that their wailing would wake up Satyavan. I saw there were two very fierce-looking dogs whose eyes burned like fire in the night. They were pawing at the gate, trying to get in... it was so frightening!' Savitri shuddered as she recounted the experience.

'Hmm...' the Kul-guru was listening with his eyes closed as he stroked his grey beard. '...and has there been anything else untoward?'

'Yes, the other morning, after Satyavan had gone to the forest, a crow suddenly flew in through the door and started cawing, all the while looking at me,' she said.

The Kul-guru opened his eyes and his gaze fell compassionately on her.

'Savitri, I know what you are going through. We both know the time is almost upon us, when Satyavan...'

'No! No! Gurudev please don't even utter that word!' Savitri's covered her ears with both hands.

'Listen to me Savitri, there is no need to panic! This is the time when you need to keep a level head on your shoulders and remain alert,' the Kul-guru said in a firm voice. 'Narad Muni had prepared all of us for this eventuality over a year ago. I know the sword of foreknowledge has been hanging over your head. I also know the enormous strength of will it has required on your part, to live with this foreknowledge that would have devastated any other woman. But I feel that by the sheer force of your will, by the depth of the love you have for your husband, you could... you just could, perhaps, change what Fate has decreed.'

'But Gurudev, I am a mere mortal subject to the laws of mortality,' said Savitri. 'How can I challenge the Lord of Death himself?'

'I believe that a human being has to rise above the confines of mortality. We are creations of the Divine will, and so there is something of the Divine within us,' said the Kul-guru. 'It is generally said that one must not tempt Fate. But nowhere is it written that one cannot, or should not, persuade Fate and bend it to our will. Hence, nothing is set in stone. If anyone can undo the writ of Fate, it is you – whom I regard as the daughter of Goddess Savitri herself – who can do it.'

'I have been a loving wife to Satyavan and a devoted daughter-in-law to his parents, Gurudev,' said Savitri. 'I love my husband more than my own life, and I will stop at nothing to make sure Lord Yama cannot claim him for his own.'

'Savitri, Lord Yama is not really as fearful as he is generally made out to be. Tell me what do you know of Yama, the God of Death?'

'I have heard that he is very fearful to behold and strikes terror in the hearts of those who do!' Savitri said with a shudder.

'Let me allay some of your fears about him, Savitri. If, at one time, a mere youth could stand up to him, I do not see why you should fear him so much,' the Kul-guru said kindly.

Chapter 23

Yama - Son of Surya

'The Vedas tell us that Yama was the first mortal who died and somehow found his way to the celestial abodes and thus, by virtue of precedence, he became the ruler of all departed souls,' the Kul-guru told Savitri. 'He is a just judge of the karma of mortals, who weighs the good and bad deeds of the dead committed during their life span on earth, and decides how they must be rewarded for the good they have done – or how they must atone for their misdeeds in the afterlife.'

'But I have heard that his messengers are most fearful to look at, and him even more terrifying to behold. Everyone is scared to even think about them,' said Savitri.

'Actually what people fear most is death, Savitri, not the image they have of Yama that has been horrendously distorted and magnified out of all proportion. This fear has made them paint a scary picture of Yama. Yes, I know, in places, the Vedas have occasionally described his skin as having a sickly green pallor and his eyes always being blood-shot. Add that to the fact he rides a strong black buffalo, carries a heavy mace held over his shoulder and he holds a thick coiled rope with a noose in his other hand – its enough to scare anyone to death! The two, four-eyed dogs that accompany him make the picture even eerier!' the Kul-guru laughed.

'So it wasn't really my imagination seeing those two dogs at night?' Savitri wondered fearfully. 'Gurudev, do you think they came as a warning of what is soon to befall us?'

To divert her mind, the Kul-guru said, 'It will be good to remember that Yama is the son of Vivasvat, god of the rising sun, known as Surya. Saranyu – goddess of the clouds – was one of the three wives of Surya. Yama has a twin sister by the name of Yami, who later became the river Yamuna. The beauteous Saranyu who had borne Revanta, also bore the twin Ashwins – one, the Divine horseman, and the other, the Divine physician.'

'Why are you telling me all this, Gurudev? How is it going to help me in my present predicament?'

'Just bear with me Savitri and try to absorb what I am saying. Now, Saranyu, unable to bear the dazzling brilliance of Surya, created a superficial entity from her shadow called Chhaya and told her to act as Surya's wife in her absence. Chhaya gave birth to two sons: Shani – ruler of the planet Saturn, and Savarni – the eighth *Manu.* She also gave birth to two daughters, Tapti and Vishti. Shani rules Saturn, which our astrologers believe casts a malefic influence, depending on which house it is placed in one's horoscope.'

'This is all becoming quite complicated, Gurudev,' said an exasperated Savitri.

The Kul-guru laughed, 'Indeed, there are as many variations as there are scriptures – the Vedas, Puranas, Upanishads, not to mention their off-shoots. However, what is important is the moral of the story, or the kernel of truth hidden therein.

'Anyway, coming back to Yama: he and Shani are responsible for judging how human beings have lived their lives on earth. Shani metes out reward or punishment according to one's deeds during one's lifetime, while Yama grants the results of one's deeds after death.'

'Oh, I didn't really know that about Shani devta! That means that Shani and Yama must be consulting one another on where to send the person, either *swarga* or *narka,*' mused Savitri.

'Well, there is also a third person in the scheme of things – Chitragupta, the Record Keeper, who maintains a record of all the deeds a human being has done in his life. In other words,

Yama goes out well-prepared when he has to visit a person whose time has come,' added the Kul-guru.

'Gurudev, I have a question: how long after a person breathes his last does it take for the soul to exit from the body and make its onward journey?'

'Savitri, according to some sources, it is said that a soul takes four hours and forty minutes for it to reach the realm of Yama. Which is why, it is said that the person should not be cremated before this time has elapsed.'

'The very name, Yama, strikes terror in everyone's heart!' Savitri remarked.

'It probably would, especially in that person's heart who has done several misdeeds in his life! But if a person has lived an upright, pious and righteous life, he would probably relate more to Yama's other name – *Dharmaraja*, Lord of Justice. After all he is an Aditya, one of the sons of Surya, and a *Lokpala*,' said the Kul-guru.

'So those who are God-fearing, pure in heart and have led virtuous lives don't really need to fear the coming of Yama,' said Savitri, more to herself, than the Kul-guru. 'Thank you for putting my mind at rest in this way, Gurudev.'

'Remember one thing Savitri, it's not just your mind that has to remain alert and steadfast when the time comes – your heart has to remain strong as well. And what I am going to say now will hopefully inspire you to maintain both presence of mind and firmness of heart in the face of what is to come.

'So contemplate on this: The Puranas tell us that Yama, although one of the most powerful controllers of life and death, is yet subordinate to the will of Rudra – an aspect of the overruling Brahman.

'Most people are familiar with the story of Markandeya, the youth who was destined to die at sixteen years of age, but was saved from Yama's noose by Shiva who appeared at that very moment to rescue his devotee from the clutches of Yama by killing the Lord of Death with his trident. Did you know that then, at the request of the other gods who pleaded that without Yama there would be chaos in the world of mortals, Shiva restored Yama to life?'

'Yes, Gurudev,' said Savitri. 'Who has not heard the bards sing of that beautiful tale? And being saved by Shiva, he was granted the boon of immortality. It is said that Markandeya still roams the earth as the beautiful youth he was at sixteen.'

'Quite so! There are other instances too!' continued the Kul-guru. 'The *Bhagavata Purana* narrates the story of one Ajamila who had done wicked things in his life. He was a thief and had abandoned his wife and children to marry a prostitute. When he lay dying, he involuntarily started chanting the name of Narayana, one of the many names of Vishnu. Actually, Narayana also happened to be the name of Ajamila's youngest son and he had in truth been calling out to him. But such is the power of the name 'Narayana' that Vishnu thought he was calling out to Him and, therefore, not only saved him from the noose of Yama, but also gave him *moksha* by forgiving all his sins.'

'So, Yama has had to submit to the wishes of Shiva, as well as Vishnu, at one time or another. Hmm, that's interesting,' said Savitri with a glimmer in her eyes.

'Yes, but remember they are gods, and not just any gods – they are Godheads of the Trinity,' said the Kul-guru. 'However, there is an instance in which neither Shiva nor Vishnu was involved. The *Katha Upanishad* narrates the tale of a youth called Nachiketa.'

'I don't recall hearing of Nachiketa,' said Savitri.

'It's really quite interesting and maybe there's something you can learn from it,' advised the Kul-guru. 'His father Vajasravas, desiring a boon from the gods, was performing a sacrifice by offering gifts that would please them. Since the wealth of a man is even now measured by the number of cows he has, Nachiketa noticed that his father was offering only the cows that were old, barren, blind or lame to the gods, while he was keeping his prized, healthy cows for himself. Wanting his father to sacrifice his best and dearest possessions, Nachiketa went up to him and said, 'I too am your dearly beloved, to which god are you going to offer me?' When his father didn't answer, he asked him again. Even then his father didn't answer.'

'Which father would want to sacrifice his son, Gurudev?' Savitri said in a perplexed voice.

'The desires of human beings are limitless, Savitri. And the egos of some rishis are so great, that nothing less than a place in Indra's heaven will satisfy them,' answered the Kul-guru. 'So, seeing his father becoming increasingly distressed, Nachiketa asked him a third time, 'Now what else have you left to give? I am here; whom are you going to offer me to, Father?'

Vajasravas, in a fit of irritation at repeatedly being asked the same question, said, 'I will offer you to Yama!'

'My God! He really said that?' Savitri was shocked.

'He did. So, the boy went to Yama's palace and, not finding him there, spent three days and three nights waiting for him without food or drink. On his return, Yama was distressed that a Brahmin guest had been kept waiting without any hospitality offered to him and impressed by Nachiketa's determination not to leave without meeting him, he offered him three boons. As the first boon, the boy asked that on his return home, his father doesn't get angry with him. The second boon he asked was to learn about the *tvam agnim swargyam adhyesi* – the heavenly fire. And, the third and last boon he asked was that Yama reveal to him the mystery of what happens after death. As much as he avoided granting Nachiketa the third boon, the boy was persistent. Impressed by the determination of the boy not to leave without learning the secret, Yama revealed the secret of immortality to him.'

'And what was that secret?' asked Savitri.

'Only Nachiketa would know!' the Kul-guru spread his hands. 'I don't know, nor does the story tell us. But Yama not only told him the secret of immortality, he presented him a golden chain as a sign of his heavenly initiation. He further named the sacred celestial fire after Nachiketa.'

'I want to know that secret, I have to know it!' Savitri said with a firmness that surprised the Kul-guru. 'Therein lies the key that may alter Satyavan's destiny.'

'You can do one thing Savitri. The *Triratra mahavrat* is a few days away. It is a fast that is very difficult to perform. If you can do that, you will have the blessings of Varuna and Mitra and our other gods.'

Chapter 24

The Triratra Fast

Four days before the hand of cruel Fate would reach across to wrench her heart, Savitri began preparations for one of the most rigorous and severe fasts that would last for three nights and three days – the Triratra vrat. Seeing Savitri get up at dawn and grinding *til seeds* and *amla* to make a paste, her mother-in-law asked, 'Savitri, what are you going to do with this paste?'

Savitri stopped what she was doing and looked up. 'Pranam, Mother. I am making a paste with which to cleanse my body before I go for my bath.'

'But why today of all days, Savitri?'

'Mother, today is *Jyeshtha Trayodashi*, and I am going to observe the Triratra fast for Satyavan. When I got married, I had made a vow to Goddess Savitri that if I got a husband who was pure of mind and had a loving heart, who honoured his father and mother by his every word and action, who shunned every falsehood and upheld the value of Truth, I would observe this fast religiously as my way of saying thanks to the Goddess.'

'But Savitri, this is an extremely rigorous fast, you will be putting a tremendous strain on yourself.'

Dyumatsena, overhearing the tail-end of this conversation as he came out of the hut to the patch of garden where the two women were talking, added, 'Yes daughter, you won't be able to withstand the rigours of such fasting for three days and three nights. Please reconsider your decision to go ahead with this fast.'

Seeing her father-in-law, Savitri covered her head with the edge of her sari and got up to touch his feet. 'With your blessings, I shall be able to complete it successfully. I cannot go back on the vow I made to the Goddess… I must fulfill it, Father.'

'Well, dear daughter, I cannot ask you to undermine the sanctity of a vow. If you have made such a vow, then we would be doing an injustice by asking you not to go ahead with it. Does Satyavan know of this?'

'Yes, I had told him of this and he also reluctantly agreed that having made my vow, I had an obligation to fulfill it.'

'So be it. You have our consent and our blessings,' said Dyumatsena and Saivya. 'Perhaps, you should also go and receive the blessings of Rishi Dalbhaya. It would be a gesture of honouring him. He has given us food and shelter in our exile, moulded and shaped the character of Satyavan and instilled in him a love for truth… Satyavan is almost like a son to him.'

'Yes, I was going to pay my respects to him after I had received your blessings,' said Savitri.

'I don't have to tell you what a difficult fast you are undertaking, my child,' Rishi Dalbhaya said with concern in his voice. 'But having observed you for nearly a year now, I would think that if anyone can do it, it is you Savitri. My blessings are with you. I will give instructions to Niranjana to allow you into the meditation hall for the three nights, and have someone posted at the door to keep a watch.'

'Thank you Rishi-dev,' Savitri bent to touch his feet and Rishi Dalbhaya placed his hand over her head in blessing.

Discarding her garments for a single drape woven of cloth made from the inner fibres of the bark of trees, Savitri began her fast partaking neither food nor water for three nights. Standing steady as a pillar in deep meditation, she invoked the Goddess and beseeched her for the strength and fortitude of spirit she would need in the next few days to meet her fate. During the day, while attending to her household duties, she only ate the boiled root of the banyan tree and sipped some water with it.

After two days, Satyavan's mother started to worry. She took him aside and said, 'Son, this fast is taking a heavy toll on Savitri. She is looking so frail. Can't you see that? How could you have agreed to let her undertake this fast?'

'Ever since we have been married, Savitri hasn't asked me for anything,' he answered. 'I really didn't know about how strict and how difficult this fast was, so I readily agreed to her request. Anyway, there is not much we can do about it now.'

'Hmm, you are right. Although she has seen to our every little need, especially that of your blind father, not once has Savitri asked anything for herself. It amazes me that a daughter-in-law can be so giving, so selfless,' remarked Saivya. 'Well, now that just the third night is left of her fast, I suppose we shouldn't say anything and let her complete it. After all, she is keeping it for your long life and prosperity.'

'Okay, Mother. I am going into the forest to pick some fruits. Savitri will need some nourishment when she breaks her fast the next day,' saying which Satyavan picked up a wicker basket and left.

Dawn crept over the hermitage, signifying the completion of Savitri's Triratra fast. Deep in contemplation of Ushas, Goddess of the Dawn, she heard a whisper close to her ear: 'You have pleased the gods with your *tapa* and *japa*, blessed daughter of Goddess Savitri. Go forth now to meet your destiny. Our blessings are with you.'

Saivya waited outside her hut for Savitri to emerge from the meditation hall of the hermitage. She had prepared a broth of sattu for Savitri to break her fast.

'Bless me Mother, that I shall be deemed worthy by the gods to merit the rewards of this fast which I have observed for Satyavan,' she said while touching Saivya's feet.

'I don't see how they could overlook your dedication and devotion, Savitri. Go now, make your offering to the *vat vriksha* and then wake up Satyavan and give him the prasad you have offered the gods.'

Chapter 25

The Fourth Day

As Savitri walked with a heavy heart towards her hut to wake up Satyavan, she saw him returning from his bath in the river and met him at the door. She quelled the heavy feeling and putting on a cheerful face welcomed him, 'You are up very early today!'

'I could barely sleep all night! You know how worried I have been about this difficult fasting you have been doing for the past three nights. Thank God it is now over!'

'Come inside, have the prasad I offered to the gods. Mother said that you were to have it first,' smiled Savitri.

'I will, but only if you also agree to have it with me,' Satyavan said. Taking a spoonful of the kheer she offered, he in turn fed her two spoonsful of it.

'Satyavan,' she said, 'today I want to ask you for something.'

'Ask, Savitri! Do you think I could ever find it in my heart to refuse you anything?'

'Today, I also want to come with you to the forest when you go to collect firewood,' she told him.

'But why today of all days, Savitri? You are looking so weak and tired after the rigorous fast you have just completed. I think you should get some sleep, rest and nourishment,' he said with some concern.

'Well, consider it my reward for having kept this fast for you. And, I am feeling quite fine, really.'

'Then it will be as you wish my dear,' Satyavan laughed indulgently.

Savitri's face lit up. 'I will also go ask your mother for her permission to come along with you this morning,' she said.

'Wait, I am also coming with you. Let me see what she has to say about it too!' Satyavan said as he bent to pick up his axe and the length of rope that lay coiled in a corner.

Entering the hut of his parents, Satyavan said, 'Mother, listen to what Savitri is saying – she wants to come with me to the forest today. Please make her see some sense, as it is she is so weak after her fast!'

'My goodness, Savitri!' said Saivya. 'Satyavan is right. Go rest in your hut.'

'Please, Mother, allow me to go with Satyavan today. I have never asked you or dear father for anything for myself up until now. Please grant me this wish; I will rest in the shade of a tree while Satyavan collects wood.'

Dyumatsena, overhearing Savitri's plea came forward and placed his hand on Savitri's head. 'Saivya, allow Savitri to go with Satyavan. It's the first time she has asked us for something, and we should not find it in our hearts to refuse.' Then turning to his son, he said, 'Take Savitri with you son. See, she is looking so forlorn. It will do her good to be in the invigorating air of the forest.'

'Alright,' Saivya nodded her head and smiled. 'Here, Savitri, take this bundle of flatbreads I have baked. There is also some eggplant preparation and pickle I have packed along with it. Satyavan, I am sure, can pluck some wild apples and berries for you in the forest!'

Satyavan looked at Savitri and extending his hand said, 'Come then, dear wife, let us go.' Turning towards his parents, he said, 'Mother, we shall be back by evening. Can you please prepare something special today in celebration of Savitri having completed her fast?'

As they walked along the river bank, Savitri paused often to rest. 'It seems as if I am seeing all this for the first time. It was over a year ago that I first came wandering here and stayed at the hermitage,' she told Satyavan. 'Since our marriage, there has been no time to wander. My duty was first to serve your parents, then you, and then help out at the hermitage. I yearned to see all this through your eyes and that is what I am doing now,' she added letting out a deep sigh.

'And ever since I set my eyes on you in the forest,' said Satyavan, 'I have only seen my surroundings and all there is only through your eyes, often thinking, Savitri would have loved this, Savitri would have admired that, Savitri this, Savitri that… Even when you have not been physically alongside me here, you have always been in my thoughts. Your name has silently been on my lips, with every breath that I take,' he said drawing her close to him. 'Come, let's rest awhile here.'

Savitri leaned her head on his shoulder and idly stroked his long hair that had a golden glimmer wherever the sun had bleached its silken strands. She had a sinking feeling in her heart; with the foreknowledge that this was the last day, she had to snatch some precious moments with Satyavan. Her mind was flooded with thoughts of what was to come: 'At what moment will the cohorts of Yama come?' 'How will they take Satyavan?' 'What will I tell his parents?' 'Will the tapas I have done for the past one year be of no avail?'

She felt the warmth of Satyavan's lips as he turned to whisper in her ear, 'What wouldn't I give right now to read the thoughts that are floating around in your pretty little head, Savitri! Come, the sun is rising higher in the sky, let us go into the forest. I must chop sufficient wood before it gets too hot. There is much to do today.'

On entering the forest, Savitri said, 'Take me to the tree in whose shade I first saw you reclining.'

Satyavan laughed. 'You still remember that! Even though my eyes were closed, I could feel the presence of something or someone who was radiating a powerful, magnetic energy. Come, it's just a little further away…'

Arriving at the spot, Savitri place her wicker basket down and spread a mat of bamboo rushes in a shaded spot. 'You carry on with your wood-chopping, while I go and gather some herbs and fruits. And Satyavan, please don't tire yourself out too much.'

'Alright,' he laughed. 'And you don't get pricked by thorns while picking wild berries!'

While she went around plucking wild berries and other fruits, Savitri wondered why the forest was so unnaturally quiet. No birds chirped in the trees, no bees buzzed around to collect nectar from flowers. Why did the air seem so still? With that sinking feeling in her heart becoming stronger, a sigh escaped her lips as she walked towards the stream to collect some water in a copper pot for Satyavan to quench his thirst, after he returned from the vigorous task of chopping wood.

She could hear the dull tuk-tuk sound of wood being chopped as she came back to rest under the tree. The thump-thump of her own heartbeat seemed to synchronise with that of Satyavan's deft strokes of the axe. In anticipation of his imminent return, she began to unroll a banana leaf and lay out the frugal meal of flatbreads and vegetables packed for them by her mother-in-law.

Savitri heard his measured footfall before she saw Satyavan returning carrying a bundle of firewood on his head. Perspiration dotted his forehead and the sheen of sweat glistened on his bare chest and muscled arms. Putting the bundle down, he took a deep breath and ran a finger across his brow to flick off the beads of sweat which were rolling down and stinging his eyes. Taking a deep breath he sat down.

'I could barely manage to chop the last few branches today… I suddenly felt a tiredness come over me,' he told Savitri.

'The stress of my Triratra fast has had its repercussions on you. Knowing I was awake all night, I know you haven't been sleeping well these past few nights,' she said comfortingly. Offering him a cloth she had soaked in the cool waters of the stream, she said, 'Here, wipe your sweat off with this, it will cool you down and refresh you. Once you have some food inside you, the weakness will go away.'

'I really don't feel like eating just now, Savitri. I think I have a headache coming on and it's making me feel a bit nauseous,' Satyavan said weakly.

'Alright, drink some water at least and then lie down for a while. We can eat later,' she said. Reaching out her hand, she pulled him down on the mat and placed his head on her lap. Unrolling the cloth he had tied around his head, she gently mopped the sweat that was still beading his brow. 'Close your eyes and sleep awhile,' she murmured soothingly. She began humming a tune and Satyavan's eyelids began to droop as he slipped into a slumber.

The foreknowledge she had lived with of Satyavan's span of life, during her one year of marriage, was now racing towards its stark finality. He could, any moment now, breathe his last. Surprisingly enough, the thought of its inevitability seemed to calm her. And in this state of calmness she found the firm resolve with which she was going to meet the messengers of doom. She went on humming and gently swaying her body to lull Satyavan into a deep sleep.

Chapter 26

Yama Appears

An ominous hush had fallen upon the forest. A floating cloud had moved across the sky to block out the sun. Even nature appeared to be holding its breath. Not a bird flew in the sky. Not a leaf stirred. In the deathly silence came the sound of a hooved animal slowly moving towards her. Coming alert, Savitri gently lifted Satyavan's head from her lap. His eyelids fluttered in sleep as she laid it on some folded banana leaves. Quietly, Savitri stood up to confront the animal and steer it away from her sleeping husband.

Through the thicket a majestic, crowned figure wearing red robes, sitting astride a black buffalo strode slowly towards her. She saw the heavy mace slung over one powerful shoulder, and a coiled rope with a noose at one end dangling from his other hand. A shudder ran through Savitri's body and her heart leapt to her mouth as she realised 'who' was advancing towards them. She folded her hands and respectfully bowed low in a silent greeting to Yama – the God of Death, as he approached. Involuntarily,Yama raised his hand in a blessing acknowledging her greeting.

'O gracious lady, blessed daughter of Aswapati, borne of a boon after eighteen years of rigorous tapasya in honour of Goddess Savitri, the hour appointed by immutable Fate has arrived. I have come to claim the soul of Satyavan,' saying which, Yama got off from his red-horned buffalo and adjusted his robes.

Savitri, who had quickly gathered her wits about her, now made bold to speak, 'It is a high honour you do us, Dharmaraja. I was under the impression that you sent your emissaries to collect mortal souls.'

'Satyavan is not an ordinary mortal. He is an upholder of the Truth, a highly evolved soul. He is a prince among men. Before coming today, I read the account of his life in the Book of Judgement kept by Chitragupta – the record keeper. I noted that he had lived a blameless life in exile in the devoted service of his blind father and loving mother. Never a word of complaint or rebuke has passed his lips, never a moment of pain at the loss of his inheritance. There has not been a single flaw to pick in his character, and the way he has conducted his life in this hermitage in the wilderness. His virtues have been so many, I could extol them at length. Such a soul is rare among mortals, therefore I have personally come to see in whose body it dwelt. It is with some regret that...'

Before he could continue further, Savitri broke in saying, 'Dharmaraja, you are known by all as the Lord of Justice, it is you who weighs the virtues and demerits of mortals in the balance and Satyavan, as you yourself have just said...'

'Yes, it is only after having evaluated his several virtues and seeing his noble character that I was compelled to come myself to collect his soul, and I cannot return without taking it with me,' answered Yama. 'Therefore, gentle lady, be so kind as to stand back.'

'But his breathing still hasn't stopped.'

'Yes, it did, as soon as you lifted his head from your lap and laid it on a cushion of banana leaves.'

Saying this, Yama unwound his thick rope and swung its noose towards Satyavan's limp form. Savitri's gaze followed the rope as it flew through the air, almost in slow motion it appeared, before landing softly around Satyavan's head and circling around his chest. With a gentle tug of the rope, Yama drew out Satyavan's soul, which was an *angushthamatrah purusham,* bound by the noose. She was now gazing upon the lifeless form of Satyavan that lay as if in deep sleep.

Several thoughts flew around in her head: 'What will I tell his parents when they see me returning alone?' 'How will I break the news to them? They will be devastated.' 'What if they find out I knew about this event all along?'

Hearing the rustle of leaves, Savitri turned around to see Yama moving towards his mount and the soul of Satyavan, imprisoned in the noose, being pulled behind him.

Chapter 27

The Boons of Yama

Overwhelmed with grief and with faltering steps, Savitri started walking behind Yama's retreating form as his mount lumbered southwards – the direction in which lay the abode of the dead. After they had gone some distance, Yama, hearing the footsteps of someone following him, turned around to look. Reining in his mount, he saw Savitri following him with a determined expression on her face and a new resolve in her eyes.

Yama was aghast. Leave alone stand in his presence, no human had had the courage nor dared to follow him prior to this. He was both astounded and enraged. But noticing Savitri's heartbroken, forlorn look, his eyes softened. Halting his mount, he admonished her in a gentle voice.

'Thus far and no further, Savitri. You cannot accompany your husband to the land of the dead. Return to your husband's body lying inert under the tree. Take him away to his parents so that they may lay him on the funeral pyre with appropriate prayers and rituals. Observe the period of mourning and then pick up the threads of your life again.'

'I have no intention of mourning, Yama-dev, as long as I am walking behind my husband. My place is by his side, dead or alive.'

'Savitri, by virtue of his death, you have been freed from all your obligations to Satyavan. You have come as far as it is possible to come. Now I suggest you return.'

'Yama-dev, I have led the life of an ascetic this past year in the hermitage, in the service of rishis and sages and my husband's parents. I have observed my vows religiously and I have loved and served my husband with my whole heart and entire being. The wise sages told me that by walking only seven steps with another, one establishes a bond of friendship with one's companion – as I have done with you. I have walked this far, and I shall keep walking behind you and the soul of my husband, which you have secured with your noose. You, Yama-dev, are the mighty son of Vivasvan, who deals with everyone fairly and upholds the laws of *dharma*. My place is by my husband's side – by scriptural mandate, social custom, and by the injunction of dharma. Therefore, I cannot go back without him as that would be going against my dharma,' Savitri answered.

Yama rubbed a hand over his chin and looked thoughtful. Savitri had a point and she had made it well. Yet, there was no way he could release Satyavan's soul. No way! But how could he get around this improbable situation in which he now found himself? Then a thought struck him.

'Savitri, I am impressed with the argument you have put forth. For that, I will grant you a boon. Ask me for anything except the life of your husband.'

Savitri paused to think. She knew that she had to think this out carefully if she was to accomplish what she had set out to do. So she said, 'Yama-dev, my father-in-law, bereft of his eyesight and subsequently his kingdom, has been living in exile in the refuge of Rishi Dalbhaya's hermitage. He has suffered hard and long. I wish you to end his suffering by granting him eyesight and thereby his strength, so he can reclaim the kingdom of Salwa that is rightfully his.'

'It shall be as you ask, Savitri. Now please turn back. You are weary and tired, return to the hermitage.' Having granted the boon, Yama prodded his mount and began to move on through the sylvan forest. But Savitri's reply made him stop again.

'How can I feel weary in the presence of my husband, Yama-dev?' asked Savitri. 'The fate that is my husband's is certainly mine as well. I shall follow him wherever you take him. Among the vows we had exchanged during our marriage, was the vow to always remain by his side. By following you, I am only observing that vow.'

Yama smiled. 'These words that you have spoken, Savitri, gladden my heart. They would enhance the wisdom of even the most learned of men. Ask of me another boon, except the one for Satyavan's life, and I shall be happy to grant it.'

'My father, King Aswapati, had done a rigorous tapasya for eighteen long years in the forest, and a great yagna thereafter, to beget a son. However, the Goddess Savitri, in her wisdom, bestowed on him this daughter you see standing before you today,' said Savitri. 'For my father, I ask the boon of a hundred worthy sons, born from the seed of his loins, so that his line may be perpetuated.'

'May every father have a wise, caring and loving daughter such as you, Savitri, who even in her own misery can wish for her father's happiness. I will happily grant this boon. Go now, do not persist in following the soul of your dead husband.'

'My father's happiness you have granted Yama-dev and for that I am truly grateful,' said Savitri. 'But as for asking me to return, to what shall I return – the lifeless corpse of my husband?'

'What lies there is just the shell of your husband, Savitri. His soul, which is pure, will rest comfortably in my kingdom until the record of his deeds, which no doubt have been that of a noble, obedient son and a loving husband, shall be weighed in the balance. Then, accordingly, it will be sent onwards to reside with the gods in heaven. You can rest happy with that thought,' Yama assured Savitri.

'I know he will be comfortable in your kingdom and since you are also known as the Lord of Justice, I am confident you will dispense absolute justice while evaluating his deeds. On one hand, by granting the boons I have asked for, I know you want me to fulfill my responsibilities towards Satyavan's parents and also use my remaining life on earth to some good purpose,' Savitri answered. 'But, how can I be happy when you are carrying away that which was the source of my happiness and the love of my life, with you?'

Yama took a deep breath and then let out a long sigh. 'Even love must bend to the will of Fate, Savitri. Yet, I am truly amazed at the extent of your devotion, your commitment to your husband. Never before have I encountered such courage and determination, such depth and intensity of love in a woman. It is so rare that to honour it, I will be happy to grant you one last boon. Ask for anything, but don't ask for…'

At that very moment, a doe crossed their path with a young faun in tow. It froze for a few moments to gaze at the buffalo.

It was now or never, Savitri thought. Seizing the moment, Savitri quickly said, 'Dharmaraja, I ask for the boon of a hundred sons born to me of my husband.'

His attention distracted for a moment by the presence of the doe and her faun, Yama automatically said, 'Granted!'

In one graceful movement, the doe leapt across the path, while the young faun ambled across.

Savitri's heart leapt with joy and a smile wreathed her face.

'Thank you, Yama-dev. You are indeed compassionate and benevolent.'

Yama's eyes grew wide as he realised the implications of the boon he had just granted. Wonderstruck, he stared at Savitri.

'You did not ask for Satyavan's life! Yet how will the boon see fruition, unless I release his soul! In the face of adversity, Savitri, you have displayed a remarkable force of will along with an astounding presence of mind.'

'So now I request you, Dharmaraja, for the boon of life for Satyavan. For by your words alone will he be restored to me.'

'So be it!' Saying this, Yama gently removed the noose in which Satyavan's soul was trapped. The spirit of Satyavan flew north and quickly vanished from sight.

'You have won the day,' said Yama with good cheer. 'Return now, go to him and wake him from his sleep.'

Chapter 28

Satyavan Awakens

Her heart filled with joy, Savitri sped back to the glade in the forest where Satyavan lay. Approaching the still form of her husband, she saw a king cobra who, with its hood flared, had been guarding over him. Savitri folded her hand and bowed with reverence acknowledging its protective presence. Uncoiling itself, the cobra slithered away into the grass.

Kneeling down, Savitri gently lifted Satyavan's head and placed it once again in her lap. She noticed that his chest no longer appeared to be collapsed and caved in. It was fuller now, rising and falling with the breath of life. Stroking his hair, she bent over to kiss his forehead. At the touch of her soft lips, Satyavan's eyelids flickered and he stirred awake. Tears of joy flowed down Savitri's eyes and fell over his face. She quickly wiped them away before Satyavan could notice her crying.

'That's the best sleep I have had in a long, long time,' he said looking up into Savitri's eyes. 'But you should have woken me up earlier. The sun is low in the sky. My parents will be wondering why we haven't yet returned home. What will we tell them?'

'Why, we will just tell them you overslept because you had a spell of dizziness while chopping wood,' said Savitri. 'And do you know, I had an encounter with a very wise and kind sage when I left you sleeping and went to pick fruits and berries. He had come in search of some food and I offered him some of the fruits I had picked. The sage was so pleased that he blessed me saying that all our wishes will soon come true.'

'That's something to look forward to indeed,' sighed Satyavan. 'Ever since I can recollect, we've been living in this hermitage. My father never talks of the kingdom he lost. Mother at times only talks of her maternal home.'

'Don't worry, all is going to be well now,' reassured Savitri.

'Why am I feeling so tired as if I have walked a long, long way? Oh, I must tell you that I had quite a strange dream in my sleep. I felt someone was dragging me with a rope through the forest. Then after being dragged thus for some time, the rope got loosened and I was freed. It was all so weird.'

'You were just tired felling wood in the hot sun. And that dizziness you felt naturally left you feeling a little weak,' said Savitri. 'Come, sit up now. Go bathe in the river, while I peel you some fruits to eat. Then we can look around for a cave in which we can take shelter for the night. We will leave early morning for the hermitage.'

Satyavan got up to go to the stream flowing nearby. Feeling refreshed after a bath, he returned to where Savitri had laid out fruits on banana leaves. 'I'm quite famished, you know.'

'I know you are,' Savitri smiled and then added, 'You don't want to spend the night in the forest, do you?'

'Much as I would have loved to, we just can't do that Savitri. My father and mother will be worried if we don't return home tonight. As it is we have been out in the forest for such a long time. They must be wondering whether we have run into some sort of trouble. You know how agitated they get if I am even a few minutes late.'

'But it will take us twice as long, if not more, in the dark of the night to reach the hermitage! What if we lose our way? If only we had something to light the path,' Savitri said wistfully.

'Savitri, you are forgetting that I have grown up here. I know this forest like the back of my hand. I will get you back safely, trust me,' said Satyavan. 'Soon there will be enough moonlight. What's more, by the position of the stars in the sky, I know the direction in which the hermitage lies.'

'As you wish, dear husband. Are you quite sure you wouldn't like to rest a while longer?'

'I'm really quite alright, Savitri, don't worry. Forget the wood I had chopped. I will come back tomorrow morning to pick it up. Let us just try and get back to the hermitage for now.'

'As you wish.'

'Come then, give me your hand. Look Savitri, look at those glow worms in the trees. Aren't they a lovely sight! Flickering like the lights of Ayodhya must have that night when Lord Rama returned with Sita to his kingdom.'

Chapter 29

The Miracle of Sight

'Saivya! Saivya! Come here!' Dyumatsena called out to his wife.

'What is it, husband? I am busy in the kitchen,' Saivya called back to him.

'Just leave everything and come here,' Dyumatsena insisted.

Saivya came out, wiping the flour off her hands, to see Dyumatsena rubbing his eyes vigorously.

'What's the matter? Do you need something?' she asked. 'And, why are you rubbing your eyes so hard?'

'I can't believe this... I can't believe this!' Dyumatsena said excitedly. 'Saivya, I can see!'

'Have you been dreaming? We can all see in our dreams!' she exclaimed.

'This is not a dream Saivya, I can actually see. Look, tell me, isn't that a woodpecker pecking away at the trunk of that tree? And look there – aren't those cauliflowers growing in the garden patch? See there – Satyavan's sandals.'

'What miracle is this, husband? How has your eyesight returned after these many years?'

'I don't know... I just don't know! I was sitting here with the rays of the sun warming my eyelids, when I noticed that I was seeing blurred images. As I kept blinking my eyes, my vision kept becoming clearer and clearer.'

Without listening further, Saivya ran out towards the hermitage.

'Where are you rushing off to Saivya?' Dyumatsena called after her.

'I am going to call Rishi Dalbhaya. Wait right where you are,' Saivya shouted excitedly.

The news spread fast in the hermitage. Dyumatsena saw Saivya returning with Rishi Dalbhaya along with his acolytes. He waved out to the sage and went forward to greet him. Touching the Rishi's feet he received his blessing.

Clasping Dyumatsena by the arms, Rishi Dalbhaya raised the kneeling King. 'This is wonderful news, Rajan, simply wonderful! It is indeed by the grace of the gods that your eyesight has been restored! Where are Savitri and Satyavan? They will be so thrilled to see this miracle when they return.' Turning to the acolyte, Dalbhaya instructed, 'Pranjal, go to the woods and see why Savitri and Satyavan haven't yet returned. Ask them to come immediately!'

'Rajan,' said Rishi Dalbhaya addressing Dyumatsena, 'I will also be sending our Ayurvedic vaid to check your eyes and see if he recommends any procedure you should follow to take care of your newfound sight. This is a cause for great joy for all today. Everyone should witness this miracle, including the seers and sages of the forest!'

'My own joy knows no bounds Rishi-raj. At last I will be able to see the face of my son, the face that only my fingers have traced so far! And I will be able to see my daughter-in-law Savitri, who has been caring for us so lovingly this past year,' said Dyumatsena with tears welling in his eyes.

'Shed no more tears, husband; this is a good omen,' Saivya said as she served Rishi Dalbhaya and him some rice kheer.

The stream of visitors had begun soon after. Among them were Rishi Bhardwaj, Rishi Gautama along with his closest disciple, Rishi Varadwaja, Rishi Dhaumya, Rishi Suvarchasa and other ascetics. It was an august gathering that had come to see the phenomenon of King Dyumatsena's restored eyesight. But the next question on their lips was, 'Where are Savitri and Satyavan?'

'We are wondering what has taken them so long. They had left early in the morning for the forest and should have returned by now. I just hope nothing untoward has happened,' fretted Saivya.

Rishi Suvarchasa consoled her saying, 'Why do you worry mother? A princess as noble and virtuous as Savitri can come to no harm. Being like a god-daughter of Goddess Savitri, she is always under her protection.'

'But Satyavan is a very conscientious son; he knows that even a few minutes delay in returning home will worry us no end,' Dyumatsena said.

Rishi Gautama closed his eyes for a few moments. 'With my powers of clairvoyance gained through years of tapasya, I see nothing amiss in the forest. There is no real cause for concern.' To which, his disciple vouched, 'Words uttered by my guru have never been proven to be wrong.'

'Let us send someone into the forest anyway to give Satyavan the good news. He will come running then,' suggested Saivya.

'Pranjal has already gone,' said Rishi Dalbhaya.

'I don't think there is any real need for that. Just look at the omens. Don't all of you feel a liveliness in the air? The koel is singing, and there, see how that peacock is dancing in your garden. The unexpected and sudden manner in which the King has regained his eyesight augurs auspicious tidings. Above all, don't forget mother Saivya that Savitri, who observed the rigorous Triratra vrat during Trayodashi for the well being of her husband, is with him. It is like a *kavach* that will protect Satyavan at all times.'

'Both Saivya and I thank you for your reassurances.'

Chapter 30

Resolution

When she saw Savitri and Satyavan approaching, Saivya ran forward to clasp her son in her arms. Tears streaming down her cheeks, she cried, 'What happened? Are you both alright? Why have you returned so late? We have all been so worried.'

Dyumatsena hurried towards Satyavan, 'Son, this day has been most remarkable! Come, come… come closer.' Taking his son's face in both his hands, he kept caressing it and beaming at him with unconcealed joy and pride.

Satyavan looked confused. 'What are you looking so intently at, father? It is me, your son.'

'Yes, I know it is you son, but all these years I could only hear your voice and the tread of your footsteps. Today I can see you and I cannot contain my joy!' Turning to Saivya, he exclaimed, 'My son has grown so handsome and strong, as befits a prince of Salwa!'

'What are you saying father? How can you possibly see me?'

Putting an arm around Satyavan's shoulder, Rishi Dalbhaya said, 'This day, a miracle has occurred. Your father's eyesight has been restored by the grace of the gods.'

'But how… what happened?' Satyavan was perplexed.

'We don't know how, son,' answered Saivya. 'This morning I was cooking your father's meal, when he suddenly called out to me. At first he was seeing things hazily, but then his vision gradually started clearing and soon he could see things perfectly, even at a distance.'

Savitri smiled and said, 'We should all give praise to the gods. Tomorrow we should perform a yagna to give thanks.'

'That still doesn't solve the mystery of this sudden miracle, after so many years of blindness,' said one of the sages.

'There is definitely far more to this than meets the eye,' pondered Rishi Dalbhaya. 'Savitri, can you please narrate the day's events that occurred in the forest and what led to your delay in returning to the hermitage? This surely has something to do with you, god-child!'

'Yes,' the rishis gathered there said in unison. 'We all have heard of the vow you had made to perform the severe Triratra fast, which is not possible for an ordinary woman. There has to be more to this turn of events and in all probability, you know something about it.'

All eyes turned to Savitri.

Rishi Dalbhaya turned to Jabala and said, 'Get some logs and build a bonfire here. Then bring us some refreshments. Let us gather around and hear what Satyavan and Savitri have to tell us.'

'All I can remember is that I was up in the tree chopping some branches, when I suddenly got a headache. I thought maybe it was just a touch of the sun, so I climbed down. I told Savitri my head was paining and I was feeling a bit dizzy too. I lay down under the tree and went to sleep. That is all that I remember. I don't know how long I slept,' Satyavan said shrugging his shoulders. 'When I awoke, it was already evening and that's the reason we were late coming back.'

'So you don't have any idea how your father's eyesight got restored all of a sudden?' asked Rishi Gautama.

'No, I really don't. How can I possibly know?'

Rishi Dalbhaya turned to look questioningly at Savitri. 'I wondered why you were so insistent on keeping the Triratra fast, despite all of us telling you not to undertake such a rigorous undertaking. So now I ask you for the real reason why you observed it, Savitri. You said you had made a vow to the Goddess. What was that vow?'

'Yes Savitri,' said Saivya, 'all of us need to know what has been going on.'

'Let us not compel Savitri to reveal anything that she is not permitted to,' cautioned Rishi Gautama. 'Ever since I attended her marriage to Satyavan, I have known, through the power of foresight, that she was born of a boon granted by Goddess Savitri. That explained the effulgence her form radiated and which was visible only to a select few, spiritually-advanced people. However, Savitri, if you are not sworn to reveal certain things, then I request you to unfold the sequence of events that have led to this miracle we have witnessed today.'

Savitri first glanced at her father-in-law and then looked at Satyavan. Taking a deep sigh, she began her narration:

'As everyone gathered here knows, I had come to this hermitage little over a year ago, accompanied by my Kul-guru, and sought refuge here from the disturbed state of affairs in the kingdom of Salwa. During my stay here, I met Satyavan and saw in him all the qualities that I wished for in a husband. But I did not convey by word or by any action of mine, my intention to Satyavan.

'On my return to my father's palace in the kingdom of Madra, I told him of my travels and of having chosen Satyavan to be my husband. It so happened that the messenger of the gods, Lord Narad, was visiting my father. Hearing of my choice of partner, he predicted the death of Satyavan within a year. He had then advised that I choose another. But I answered that after having accepted Satyavan with my mind and heart as my husband – it would be a sin for me to even harbour the thought of another. Therefore, I prevailed upon my father, mother and Narad Muni to accede to my heart's desire.

'Since the day of my marriage, I had known that today was the day appointed by destiny for Yama to come and take the soul of Satyavan. For one year – day and night – I had lived with this fear. This is why three nights ago, I began observing the Triratra fast in preparation for what was to come. During these three nights, I harnessed the energy of the Goddess and received the blessings of the gods in my tryst with destiny.

'I sought the permission of Satyavan's revered parents to accompany Satyavan to the forest today, as I was determined to meet Lord Yama and plead with him for the life of my beloved husband. When Yama swung his noose imprisoning the soul of Satyavan and began to take him away, I followed him at every step. Upon being asked to turn back repeatedly by Yama, since I, a living soul, could not enter the realms of the dead, I kept refusing to turn back. Yama kept granting me boon after boon – restoration of eyesight for my father-in-law along with the restoration of his kingdom; a hundred sons for my father King Aswapati who, despite his tapasya of eighteen years, had not been granted the son he had wished for but instead been given this daughter you see before you today. Finally, I asked for the boon of a hundred sons for me and Satyavan, which Yama-dev in a moment of distraction, hurriedly granted.

'Well, it was natural then for me to ask for Satyavan to be restored back to life as without him, the last boon Yama gave me could not have been fulfilled. Pleased with my spiritual attainments, my devotion to my husband and his parents, the severe austerities and the ascetic life I have led this past one year, the good Lord Yama also has granted a life of four hundred years for Satyavan and continued prosperity of his lineage.

'Such is the truth as I have narrated to this august gathering of revered rishis and sages.'

Everyone gathered there had listened spellbound to how Savitri had upheld the vow and virtues of a truly devoted wife.

Rishi Dalbhaya rose to say, 'Savitri, by the unflinching observance of your vows, you have turned the misfortunes of King Dyumatsena, foremost of kings, into good fortune and ensured the continuance of his bloodline and dynasty for generations to come. I bow to such a virtuous woman who has not only upheld the dharma, but has set an example for all women to emulate – as a wife, as a daughter, as a daughter-in-law and above all, you have shown us how a woman, possessed of strong will and determination, can rise to become a master of her own destiny.'

Queen Saivya, whose eyes had welled with tears listening to Savitri's tale of forebearance, fortitude and selfless sacrifice, came forward to envelop her in a loving embrace. 'Blessed we are to have a daughter-in-law as you... for with your spiritual practices, virtues and devotion, you have accomplished miracles and ensured a happy end to our exile.'

Dyumatsena, with folded hands, added to Saivya's words: 'Savitri, even a daughter could not have done more than what you have for us. A deep regret had lain heavy on me and Saivya all these years in exile, which we had always strived to hide from young Satyavan. That was the fact that due to my blindness, his birthright had been snatched from him and he would be left with nothing.'

Then turning to look at Rishi Dalbhaya, he said, 'If it had not been for the kindness of Rishi-dev here, I do not know how we would have survived all these years. His spiritual strength, moral support and guidance helped us brave all odds.'

He looked at Savitri adoringly and added, 'Then last year you came, sent by the gods I'm sure, to change our lives. You came as a ray of sunshine that helped dispel the dark solitude of my blindness. You brightened our days with your outpouring of love, regard and affection on all of us. And now you have secured Satyavan's birthright for him. Dearest daughter, I humbly bow...'

Savitri clasped both his hand in hers. 'Father, dear Father...' she said. 'Please... please... it is not fitting that you stand with folded hands before me. You are as beloved to me as my own parents. Whatever has occurred, has come to us with the blessings of the gods, and the goddess Savitri. It is to them we owe our gratitude and thanks.'

Saivya went up to her son and caressed his head. 'Cherish her dearly, Satyavan,' she said looking fondly at him. 'You have indeed been blessed to have such a devoted and loving life-partner as Savitri. Hold her close to your heart – now and forever more. A woman of unrivalled virtues such as our Savitri will continue to shine as a beacon of love, courage and compassion throughout the ages.

Chapter 31

Jubilation

The hermitage woke to the sound of trumpets, drumbeats and the clanging of cymbals next morning. Startled, Rishi Dalbhaya along with the inmates of the hermitage rushed out and saw ministers and courtiers of the kingdom of Salwa approaching the gates of the ashram. They held aloft the royal banners and pennants emblazoned with the insignia of King Dyumatsena.

'Jabala, go and open the gates,' Rishi Dalbhaya told the acolyte.

A senior minister of the court, whom Rishi Dalbhaya recognised as once having served under King Dyumatsena, came forward to receive the sage's blessing.

'Greetings, Rishi-dev,' he said bowing low.

'Welcome Raj-guru, it's so good to see you. What brings you here along with these courtiers, today?' enquired the Rishi.

'It's a day of rejoicing in Salwa, Rishi-dev. In a coup mounted by some loyalists of King Dyumatsena, the pretender to the throne of Salwa was overthrown and assassinated along with his coterie yesterday. We have come to welcome our beloved King Dyumatsena back to the throne of Salwa. Whether possessed of sight or not, the people want him as their king because they were happy and prospering under his benign rule.'

'The gods be praised!' said Rishi Dalbhaya. 'I also have some good news for you. King Dyumatsena has regained his eyesight completely. Come, I shall take you to him and you can see for yourself!'

Beholding their king, the ministers and the courtiers bowed to him.

'Greetings King Dyumatsena and Queen Saivya of Salwa,' they intoned. 'The usurper to your throne has been overthrown and the Council has unanimously proclaimed our rightful Lord Dyumatsena – the King of Salwa – once again! The kingdom and its citizens eagerly await your return to the capital. The royal chariot awaits your pleasure.'

'It will have to wait awhile,' said Dyumatsena. Then turning to Rishi Dalbhaya, he requested him to gather all the sages and seers dwelling in the forest along with their disciples. Before leaving, he wanted to thank them for their gracious support to him during these long years in exile. Saivya also wished to perform a yagna in honour of the gods who helped create the circumstances that had led to this providential turn of events.

Gathered around the fire of the yagna were the King and Queen along with the heir apparent Prince Satyavan and Princess Savitri. The Rishis Dalbhaya, Bhardwaja, Gautama, Suvarchasa, Varadwaja and Dahuma chanted mantras and hymns in praise of the gods, while the royals poured offerings of ghee, grains, and fruits into the sacrificial fire. The flames leapt up towards the skies indicating that the gods had accepted their offerings and were pleased.

Dressed now in their royal robes, Dyumatsena and Saivya sought the blessings of the sages to ensure a happy and prosperous reign, and invited them all to attend the coronation ceremonies which would be held in the capital a few days from now.

The banners of Salwa were fluttering gaily in the breeze, a sure sign that the god Varuna was overjoyed. Mounting the royal chariot, they bid their last goodbyes and took leave of Rishi Dalbhaya and the inmates of his hermitage. Satyavan rode a white stallion alongside the chariot carrying his parents, while Savitri was borne in a silver palanquin by liveried guardsmen.

As the royal entourage rode along the harbour, there were cheers from the fishing boats and the merchant traders.

Streamers and flags bearing the royal insignia fluttered gaily from the city's ramparts. The gates of the city had been flung wide open and people lined the streets to shower rose petals on the royal family who waved to the men, women and children as their chariot made its way to the palace.

On the day appointed by the court astrologers as being auspicious, a great yagna was performed to thank the gods for this happy turn of events. Then the coronation of King Dyumatsena took place, at which Satyavan was announced as the crown prince, amid great pomp and ceremony.

Dyumatsena in his coronation address to the people of Salwa said:

'I have returned as your king thanks to the boons granted to my daughter-in-law Savitri, a princess of great virtue and piety, who with her loving dedication lived up to every expectation and more during our exile. Born herself as a boon to her parents by the Goddess Savitri, she is a living example to all womanhood of what a person who possesses a strong, indomitable will and courage can achieve. She can even compel the gods to alter the course of human destiny.

'Today, we also enshrine the image of Goddess Savitri, in a temple dedicated to her honour, as the presiding deity of our kingdom. All who pray to her with a heart as pure as Savitri will receive her protection and blessings.'

'Let us all rejoice and pledge to make Salwa one of the most prosperous kingdoms in this land.'

The sage Markandeya concluded his tale
to King Yudhishtra, saying:

'Thus, O son of Pritha, did Savitri rescue from misfortune and exile, and raise to great fortune and glory her own and Satyavan's parents...

...as well as procure sons for herself and her husband – the sons who would rule for generations to come. In doing so, she also secured the future prosperity of both the kingdoms of Madra and Salwa.

And like Savitri, whose virtue is beyond compare, so will Draupadi, the daughter born from the flames of King Drupad's yagna, prove to be your saviour when the great battle of Mahabharata is fought... and won.'

Epilogue

The Mahabharata states that Savitri went on to have one hundred sons. So did her father, Aswapati, also begat a hundred sons as a result of the boon.

The kingdom of Salwa became a power to be reckoned with under successive kings. It had a formidable navy comprising a large fleet of ships. It offered a large, well-equipped harbour for merchant ships of various nations of Asia Minor and particulary to Greece and Macedonia in Europe. It provided the most accessible sea-route for trade to the kingdoms of Kuru and Panchala among others of the north-western and central regions.

– Mahabharata-Vana Parva, Ch. 291-298,
Maharaja of Burdwan's edition.

Notes

The story of Savitri and Satyavan is one of the best-known and best-loved tales of India. It appears within the great epic Mahabharata and is narrated by Markandeya – the immortal sixteen-year-old sage – to King Yudhishtra of the Pandava clan.

The Mahabharata, orally passed on for centuries, is generally thought to have been written down around 540 BCE – 300 BCE. The epic arises from a time when legends were born – an age of walled cities, of sun and fire worship, and of women far more independent than later Indian culture would allow them to be.

The legend of Savitri and Satyavan has been told and retold through the form of epic, poetry, drama, opera, television and cinema – at home and abroad. Some of these are:

Savitri – A Legend and a Symbol, Sri Aurobindo.

Savitri Satyavan – Silent film by Dadasaheb Phalke, 1914.

Savitri – A ballet performed by renowned danseuse and film actress Hema Malini.

The legend of Savitri and Satyavan has been made into several regional films and TV serials.

Overseas:

Savitri – A chamber opera in one act by Gustav Holst performed first at Wellington Hall, London in 1916.

Savitri, or Love and Death – A poem by Edwin Arnold.

Savitri: Dance in the Forest of Death, performed by Thresh, Columbia College, Dance Centre, Chicago, July 12, 2013 at the Taiwan International Festival of the Arts.

Savitri Satyavan – India's first international Indo-Italian co-production directed by Giorgio Mannini, 1923.

Savitri and Satyavan in Indian folk art

A representative scene from the legend of Savitri and Satyavan as depicted in this Madhubani Painting – one of the oldest art forms from the Mithila region of Bihar.

– Photo reproduced by permission of Sandhya Arvind

Chapter 1

Aswapati or Ashwapati means 'Lord of the Horse'. Asva or Ashwa, the Horse, is a Vedic symbol of the Life-Energy force, complementary to the cow, which represents a ray of light.

The Kings of Madra and Kekaya usually went by the title of 'Ashwapati'. Kautilya mentions that the chief of the Madra tribe was generally addressed by the title of Rajasabdopajivinah, Raja or 'Rajan' for short, to refer to a king.

Malavi was a princess of Malava, a minor tribal kingdom neighbouring the Madra region. Much later, the tribe migrated and became powerful as the Malavas of Central India, in what is today known as Madhya Pradesh.

Vaids and *hakims:* Ayurvedic doctors and physicians

Kul-guru: Kul – clan; guru – teacher

Pranam: Traditional greeting

Ayushman bhava: May you live long

Tapasya: Penance

Mahayagna: Maha – great; yagna – ritual fire sacrifice

Jo aagya Gurudev: As you say, dear Guru

Brahmacharya: Vow of celibacy

Chapter 2

Chola: Loose cloth wrapped around the body, usually worn by ascetics

Sattu: A mixture of cereals and pulses; in this case a sweet delicacy made of this mixture

Kamandal: A water-pot carried by ascetics

Khadawa: Wooden footwear

Savitr: The effulgent phase of the rising sun

Bhoja patra: Leaf of the Bhoja tree

Chapter 3

Rishi Dalbhaya, son of Rishi Chikitayan, is first mentioned as having an ashram at Ayodhya in the reign of King Yuvanasva II of Ayodhya. When his son Mandhata succeeded the throne around 5828 BCE, he embarked on a series of conquests over neighbouring kingdoms, finally even conquering Gandhara in present-day Afghanistan. Mandhata is said to be the first monarch to gain the title of Emperor.

Rishi Dalbhaya finally emerges again during the exile of King Dyumatsena of Salwa, when the king seeks refuge in his ashram in the wilderness on the outskirts of Salwa. [*History of Ancient India: From 7300 BCE to 4250 BCE,* J. P. Mittal]

Banjaras: Gypsies

Mohurs: Gold currency

Amavasya: Night of the new moon

Dhatura: The Jimson weed plant; its leaves are used as an intoxicant

Kayasatha: The Chandraseniya Kayastha Prabhus of today trace their origins to Queen Kamala's son, Kayastha. They are known to combine the qualities of the penetrating intellect of the Brahmin, along with the fidelity and courage of the Kshatriya warrior

Chitrasen: Satyavan was also occasionally referred to by the names Chitrasen and Chitraswa, as he was fond of painting

Chapter 4

Pancha kosas: The five subtle sheaths

Ajna chakra: Third-eye chakra, located in the brow, is the sixth primary chakra according to Hindu tradition

Siddhis: Powers that arise within the person with the rigorous practice of yoga

Chapter 5

Vanaras: A tribe of forest dwellers, usually associated with Bali, Sugriva and Hanuman

Kutir: Hermit's hut

Chapter 6

Prasad: Consecrated offering of sweet preparations made to the god which is infused with sacred energy and distributed to the devotees

Chapter 7

Dhoop: Incense made from paste of fragrant spices

Gayatri mantra: Mantra of the sun

Sura wine: Intoxicating drink

Chapter 8

Samskaras or Sanskaras are rites of passage in a human being's life described in ancient Sanskrit texts, as well as a concept in the karma theory of Indian philosophy. They imply a 'putting together, making perfect, getting ready, to prepare'.

In the context of karma, Sanskaras are dispositions, character or behavioural traits, which are present from birth as a result of genes and conditioning, or inculculated and perfected by a person over one's lifetime, that exist as imprints on the subconscious mind. These influence and shape a person's nature, responses, and states of mind.

Chapter 9

The legendary beauty of Madra women, like those from the northwest kingdom of Kamboja, has been well-documented. They were fair-complexioned; in fact, they are termed as 'white' in the Mahabharata. – *Journal and Proceedings of the Asiatic Society of Bengal, 1927*.

Savitri was renowned for her beauty among the kings and princes of the neighbouring kingdoms and beyond.

Madri, the sister of King Shalya of Madra, was married to Pandu, the Kuru prince of Hastinapur. Bhishma, the father-like figure of King Pandu of the Kuru clan, had gone to the capital city of Sakala of Madra, to ask for King Shalya's sister, Madri, as a bride for Pandu. Shalya told him: 'There's a *shulka*, a custom in our family observed by our ancestors, which be it good or bad, I am incapable of transgressing it. It is well-known, and therefore is known to thee as well, I doubt not. The custom is the groom has to give dowry to the kinsmen of the bride.' Thus Bhishma gave much wealth to Shalya and took Madri as a bride for Pandu. (Mahabharata, Adiparva, Ch. 1, 113).

The *Sumagala Vilasini* tell us that the bride of a Chakravarti king comes either from Uttara Kuru or from Madra.

Prabhavati, a princess of Madra, was married to prince Kusa, son of Okkaka, of the Ikshvaku royal family of Benares (Jataka – Cowel, Vol. V, pp 146-147).

According to Mahavamsa, on the death of King Sihabahu of Sinhapura (Lata Rashtra = Gujarat), his son Summita became king of Lata Rashtra. He married a Madra princess by whom he had three sons.

Khema, one of the three queens of King Bimbisara of Haryanka dynasty (544-491 BCE), ruler of Magadha, was a princess of Madra.

Chapter 10

In the Madra social structure, women were treated equal to men and there was no taboo of social mixing among the sexes. Women also took part in matters of polity and civic administration.

– *The Culture and Civilization of Ancient India in Historical Outline, p. 119 D. D. Kosambi.*

Devakanyeti: Daughter of the gods – a term used for Savitri in the Mahabharata.

Swayamvara: The rite of 'Swayamvara' in which a maiden chose her own husband. It was practiced and sanctioned by religion and socially accepted in Vedic times:

'*Swayam anviccha bharatarm gunaih sadrsam atmanah*': 'Choose the husband for yourself, equal to your own qualities,' says Aswapati to his daughter in the Mahabharata re-telling of the story.

Chapter 11

Akshaya Tritiya: A holy day for Hindus and Jains. It falls on the third Tithi (lunar day) of Bright Half (Shukla Paksha) of the Indian month of Vaishakha (April-May), and is one of the four most important days for Hindus

Chapter 12

Kamarband: A strip of cloth tied around the waist

Kama deva: Hindu god of love

Chapter 13

The story of Shakuntala is narrated in the Adi Parva and Sambhava Parva of the Mahabharata. One of the most popular legends of love and romance, it was romanticised by Kavi Kalidasa in his popular play *Abhijñānaśākuntala* – 'The Sign of Shakuntala'. The romance inspired the performing arts, the world over: an opera by Schubert, ballets by Ernest Reyer and Sergey Balasanyan and , the Norwegian musician, Amethystium, wrote a song called 'Garden of Sakuntala'. Closer home, films on the theme were made by Bhupen Hazarika and V. Shantaram.

Gandharva: The rite in which a man and a woman marry by exchange of garland in front of a temple deity as witness

Chapter 15

Narad Muni: Divine messenger and a god who travels bearing news between the three worlds

Prithvi lok: Earth

Phalgun: Month of April

Jnani: Realised being

Upaaya: Solution

Dosha: Fault

Chapter 16

The most renowned of the celestial devotees of Narayan or Lord Vishnu as he is more popularly known, Narad, besides being musically gifted, was also widely respected as the orator of the *Naradsmrti*, referred to as the 'juridical text par excellence' by sages and scholars alike. Blessed with a silver-tongue combined with a pleasing manner, he was not only very eloquent but also possessed high intelligence and a resolute will.

According to the scriptures, Narad Rishi is the son of Brahma and Saraswati. This makes him the grandson of Vishnu as Brahma came forth from the navel of Lord Vishnu. Popular as the Divine minstrel and messenger of the gods, Narad traverses the three worlds of gods, humans and asuras.

Narad had mastered Sankhya Shastra, the science of numerology and Yoga systems of philosophy. He was conversant with the science and intricacies of politics, war and treaties. In critical situations, his knowledge is put to good use by gods, humans and asuras to arrive at the right course of action.

The foremost devotee of Vishnu, as he always keeps chanting 'Narayana... Narayana...' he is said to be the originator of the Bhakti mode of worship. The Bhakti Sutras of Narad and the Bhakti Mimansa of Shandilya are considered the most authoritative ancient Sanskrit texts on Bhakti literature.

The Narad Bhakti Sutra besides being considered an authoritative scripture, is remarkable for its simplicity and clarity, a quality that is that is usually quite rare in the ancient texts.

There is a temple dedicated to the Divine sage Narad in Chigateri, about 50 km from Davanagere in Karnataka. Another temple dedicated to him at Korva, a scenic island also popularly known as Naradagadde. Its exquisite location draws not only devotees of the sage Narad Muni, but also tourists to this beautiful spot.

Chapter 18

Muhurat: Auspicious time

Angarakha: Upper garment

Chapter 20

Alta: Alta, Mahawar, or Rose Bengal, is a red dye which women in India (specially Rajput, Bengali and Oriya women) apply with cotton on the border of their feet during marriages and religious festivals. There is a tradition that after the wedding ceremony, when the bride enters her in-laws house for the first time, she steps in a plate of alta before crossing the threshold with her right foot, leaving red footsteps behind her. After entering the house, she dips both her palms in the dye and imprints them on the wall of the house.

Havan kund: Vessel for lighting the sacred fire into which offerings and oblations are poured

Rangoli: Ornamental design made of coloured powders

Mandap: A covered structure with pillars (usually of four banana trees signifying the four directions) erected for the purpose of a traditional Hindu wedding

Apsara: Heavenly maiden of Indra's court

Akhand saubhagyawati raho: May you have a long, happy and prosperous married life

Ghagra: A loose skirt

Thali: A flat wooden or metal platter

Chapter 23

Vivasvat was the Vedic version of the latter day Hindu god Surya. He was originally known as Martanda, a son of Aditi.

Surya had three wives – Saranyu, Ragyi and Prabha. Saranyu was the mother of Vaivasvata Manu (the seventh, i.e. present Manu) and the twins Yama (the Lord of Death) and his sister Yami. Saranyu also bore him the twins known as the Ashvins, Divine horseman and physician to the Devas. But unable to bear the extreme radiance of Surya, Saranyu created a superficial entity from her shadow called Chhaya and instructed her to act as Surya's wife in her absence.

Chhaya mothered two sons – Savarni Manu (the eighth, i.e. next Manu) and Shani (the planet Saturn), and two daughters – Tapti and Vishti. Surya also has two more sons – Revanta with Ragyi, and Prabhata with Prabha.

Surya is also the father of the famous tragic hero Karna, described in the Mahabharata, by a human princess named Kunti.

Manu: The first man

Moksha: Salvation, liberation

Swarga: Heaven

Narka: Underworld, the Indian equivalent of hell

Lokpala: Civil administrator

Brahman: The supreme experience of godhood, the Impersonal Absolute God

Tvam agnim swargyam adhyesi: The sacred heavenly fire

Triratra mahavrat: A fast of three nights

Chapter 24

Til seeds: Sesame seeds

Amla: Indian Gooseberry

Jyeshtha Trayodashi: Auspicious night

Tapa: Deep meditation

Japa: Reciting of mantra

Vat vriksha: Banyan tree

Chapter 26

Angushthamatrah purusham: Thumb-size human figure

Chapter 27

Dharma: Duty or moral law – a key concept with multiple meanings in Hinduism, Buddhism, Sikhism and Jainism

Chapter 29

Kavach: Protective mantra

Appendix 1

Paths to Immortality

The Brahmanas, the Vedas, the Puranas and the Epics all contain several myths of humankind's eternal quest for immortality. Here we come across stories of kings, princes, sages and devotees either hankering for the immortality that has been bestowed on the *devas* or gods, or being saved from a preordained death and granted an extended lifespan and, in some cases, the ultimate boon of immortality.

Let us briefly take a look at the circumstances in which some of these persons were thus blessed.

Trishanku's lust for immortality

The *Ramayana* tells us about Trishanku, also known as Satyavrata, who was the king of Ayodhya. After he handed over the throne to his son Harishchandra, he wanted to ascend to heaven in his mortal body. Upon asking his Kul-guru, Vashishta, to help him fulfill his ambition, he was told by the sage that this was impossible to achieve by a mortal being.

However, a sage called Vishwamitra, a rival of Vashishta's knowledge and super powers, saw an opportunity to put him down and, at the same time, ingratiate himself in the eyes of the King by coming forward to help him gain access to heaven. As a result of his years of tapasya and the special yagna he performed to enable this mission, both he and the King arrived at the gates of heaven but were turned away. King Trishanku was disheartened. Vishwamitra was furious at this insult to his years of tapasya. He decided to create a separate heaven for the

King, his own version of heaven that would exist between the heaven of the gods and the earth.

The gods of Indralok were furious and hurled him out. Trishanku fell upside down and hung suspended between heaven and earth in the in-between space dotted by stars and constellations created for him by Vishwamitra. Thus he hung for millennia, until Brahma, taking pity on his plight, and Trishanku penitent of his overriding ambition to rival the gods, ultimately granted him entry into heaven.

Nachiketa and the secret of death

The Katha Upanishad narrates the tale of Nachiketa, son of the sage Vajasravas who desiring a boon from the gods began donating all his possessions. But when it came to cows, his son noticed that his father was only giving away the cows that were old, barren, lame or blind. Now only Nachiketa remained, so the son asked his father that 'I too am yours Father, to whom will you offer me' Speechless at the child's question, Vajasravas didn't answer. But, Nachiketa kept pestering him until agitated, his father said, 'I will give you to Yama!'

So Nachiketa went to Yama. On arriving at his palace, the boy found that Yama was not there. So he stayed outside the gates for three days and three nights. When Yama returned, he was pained to see that a Brahmin boy had been kept waiting so long without being offered any hospitality. To make up for this lapse, he told Nachiketa to ask for three boons. Nachiketa first asked that when he returned to earth, his father should not get angry on him. Yama agreed. The boy then asked to be taught the sacred fire sacrifice, which also Yama granted. For the third boon, Nachiketa asked that the mystery of what comes after death to be revealed to him.

Yama hesitated and said this was a mystery even to the gods. He asked the boy to ask for some other boon, offering the inducement of material gains and riches. But the boy refused saying that for one who has encountered death, how can he desire wealth? He wanted no other boon. The answer so pleased

Yama that he elaborated on the nature of the true Self which persists after death. Thus having learnt the secret wisdom of the Brahman, Nachiketa was freed from the cycle of births. Yama then also gifted him a golden chain as the sign of his heavenly initiation and named the triple celestial fire after Nachiketa.

Markandeya – forever a youth of sixteen years

The *Skanda Purana* gives us the glorious tale of Markandeya, the son that was given by Lord Shiva as a boon to the childless Rishi Mrikandu and his wife Marudvati. Before granting the boon, Shiva asked them whether they wanted an exceptionally intelligent and pious son who would live for only sixteen years, or an ordinary child with average intelligence who would have a long life. Both Mrikandu and his wife asked the Lord to grant them the son of exceptional intelligence and piety. They were then blessed with the birth of Markandeya.

The child grew up to be a highly gifted boy well-versed, at an early age, in the scriptures and shastras. As the lad approached his sixteenth year, he noticed that his parents had begun to look very morose and forlorn. When Markandeya asked the cause of their misery, the father hesitantly revealed the boy's destiny to him. The boy told them not to worry as Shiva loved his devotees and the Puranas stated that the Lord had saved many from death.

Markandeya formed a Shivalinga near the seashore and began worshipping it day and night, chanting the Mahamrityunjya mantra all the while. The day he turned sixteen, Yama, Lord of Death, came riding on his black buffalo. Seeing him, Markandeya threw his arms around the Shivalinga and clung to it praying to Shiva for protection. Yama, without a second thought, threw the long noose that fell around the boy's neck as well as around the Shiva lingam. Tightening the noose, Yama began to drag the boy, along with the lingam, away.

Seeing this, Lord Shiva was enraged that Yama dared to throw the noose around His form and He emerged in a fiery blaze of light. He thundered at Yama saying how dared he touch even a hair of a devotee engaged in His worship! He threw His trident at Yama and killed him on the spot. He then blessed Markandeya with eternal life, proclaiming he would forever remain sixteen. Lord Shiva, on the pleas of the devas, then also restored Yama to life.

How the Savitri tale is different from other immortality tales

Savitri is unique among all the women narrated in the Vedas, Puranas, Upanishads, and the Indian epics. She embodies not just the complete dedication and love for her husband, which all epic heroines display, but also the power of absolute will and action. Like Sita, Shakuntala and Draupadi, she is also a victim of circumstances but unlike the others, she does not seek or ask for help from without to free herself and her husband from death and doom.

When Deva-rishi Narad Muni forecasts the death of Satyavan and proclaims that 'this fate of Satyavan cannot be undone by whatever means' – then that must be so. We expect it to happen just the way he has predicted. It comes as a surprise when we see that the prediction is not fulfilled. In fact, unchangeable Fate itself gets changed, which is rare for the epic form and content.

Savitri has to engage with the Lord of Death. This is the only tale in which Fate is changed 'by an unchanging will'. In the case of Markandeya, the change is brought about by Lord Shiva. In the case of Savitri, it is accomplished by the power of her own will and determination. It is this feature alone that makes the legend of Savitri and Satyavan unique, and not just her *'pativrata'* or the love and dedication extolled in later Indian tradition, which she has for her husband Satyavan.

What's also different here is that Savitri does not seek immortality – neither for herself nor for her husband. All she wants is an 'extended lifespan' for Satyavan so he can fulfill his obligations – towards his parents by reclaiming the lost kingdom for his father, towards his predecessors by enabling them to be reborn through the birth of his own sons from Savitri, and the responsibility he would have towards Salwa and its people, when he would rule as its king.

Aspects of immortality

Some immortals find their place in heaven. Other immortals blessed with eternal life are always present on earth in every *yuga* or cycle. They are known as the 'Cheeranjivis' and besides Markandeya, the other immortals are Parashurama, Hanuman, Vibhishna, Mahabali, Kripacharya and Ved Vyasa.

Then there is another kind of immortality which is not of the physical form or body. This is the immortality a person earns for his literary genius, political acumen, spiritual attainment, etc. that lingers in public memory and goes down in the annals of history. Some examples of people who have achieved such immortality include Alexander the Great, Akbar the Great, Beethoven, Elizabeth I, Shakespeare, Sai Baba of Shirdi, to name a few, who will live in public memory for generations to come.

Note:

The Katha Upanishad, while narrating the story of Nachiketa, says that Yama, pleased with Nachiketa's reply, then elaborated on the nature of the true Self, which persists beyond death. The key of the realisation, he said, is that this Self (within each person) is inseparable from Brahaman – the supreme spirit, the vital force of the universe.

Yama's explanation is a clear exposition of Hindu metaphysics, and focuses on the following points:

- The sound of the word 'Om' is the syllable of the supreme Brahman
- The Self, whose symbol is *Om,* is the same as the omnipresent Brahman. Smaller than the smallest and larger than the largest, the Self is formless and all-pervading.
- The goal of the wise is to know this Self.The Self is like a rider; the horses are the senses, which he guides through the maze of desires.
- After death, it is the Self that remains; the Self is immortal.
- Mere reading of the scriptures or intellectual learning cannot realise Self
- One must discriminate the Self from the body, which is the seat of desire.
- Inability to realise Brahman results in one being enmeshed in the cycle of rebirths. Understanding the Self leads to moksha
- Thus having learnt from Yama the wisdom of the Brahman, Nachiketa was freed from the cycle of births.

Appendix 2

Yama

In Hindu mythology, Yama is a Lokapala and an Aditya. He is son of Surya and the twin brother of Yami, traditionally considered the first human pair in the Vedas. Surya's two sons, Shani and Yama, are both judges. Shani gives the results of one's deeds *during* one's life through appropriate rewards and punishments, while Yama grants the rewards or punishments of one's deeds *after* death. Yama is assisted by Chitragupta, the record-keeper, who keeps a complete account of a person's deeds throughout his mortal life on earth. Upon the person's death, Yama decides whether his soul is to be reincarnated as a superior or as an inferior being, depending on the karma accrued during his span of life.

In the *Rig Veda*, Yama is said to be the son of Vivasvat (Surya) and Saranya, daughter of Tvastar, and having a twin sister named Yami. He is considered to be the first mortal who died – the path which all humans have since had to follow. Appointed as the Lord of Death, he is the guardian of the geographical direction that represents the South, which is considered the region of death. The Vedas describe him as a pleasant king of departed ancestors, and not as a punisher of sins. However, in later Hindu mythology, he also became known as Dharmaraja (the just Judge) who weighs the good and bad deeds of the dead in a balance and decides on rewards and punishment.

He is often described as being dark-complexioned and wearing red garments. His vehicle is a powerful black buffalo.

He holds a *pasa* (noose) in one hand and a mace or in some accounts a *danda* (iron rod) in the other. In the Garuda Purana (2.8. 28-29), he is addressed by seven names: Yama, Dharmaraja, Mrtyu, Antaka, Vaivasvata, Kala, and Sarva-pranahara.

Unswerving in his purpose of maintaining and adherence to harmony, it is said that he is one of the wisest of the gods. In the Rig Veda (10.21.5), Yama is closely associated with Agni, god of fire who is the conductor of the dead. Agni is Yama's priest who burns the dead.

In the Puranas, Yama, although one of the more powerful gods, is still subordinate to Shiva and Vishnu (with the exception of his encounter with Nachiketa) as can be gauged from the stories of Markandeya when Shiva intervened to save his devotee.

The Bhagavata Purana recounts Yama's submission to Vishnu in the story of Ajamila, a wicked man who committed evil acts during his life. He was a thief who had abandoned his wife and children and married a prostitute. When he was dying, he kept chanting the name of Narayana (one of the many names of Vishnu) and thus attained moksha by being saved from the clutches of Yama's *dutas* (messengers), Although Ajamila had actually been calling out to his youngest son, (who was also named Narayana), the name had such a powerful effect that it released Ajamila of his sins.

Not commonly known is the interesting legend of the birth of Yudhishtra: Yama, also known as Dharamaraja (Lord of Judgement), was the first god to be invoked by Kunti, wife of King Pandu who was unable to father a child, to father her son Yudhishtra – eldest of the five Pandava brothers.

Appendix 3

The Vat Savitri Vrat

A festival observed to this day

The festival of *Vat Purnima* (or Vat Savitri) is popularly celebrated in Odisha and the northern states of India, in the month of Jyeshtha (May-June) by married Hindu women who observe the fast in honour of Savitri. This fast is kept for the well-being, good health, and long life of their husbands.

Vat Savitri Vrat fasting is for three days and it begins on the Trayodashi day and ends on Purnima. Some sections of Hindu society observe the vrat during Amavasya (new moon) and others during Purnima (full moon) in the Hindu month of Jyeshtha. The number of days the fast is observed depends on the person who is observing it. Nowadays, many women, finding it difficult to keep the fast for three days, only observe it on Purnima.

Dressed in ornate bridal garments and jewellery, women fast either for three nights, or for just the third night till the next morning. Forming a group, the women offer prayers to and worship the vat (banyan) tree by offering water, rice, flowers and incense to the tree, sprinkling *kumkum* (vermillion powder) on it and wrapping a *mauli* (vermilion cotton thread) around the tree's trunk while doing the *parikrama* (circumambulation) seven times around it. Sitting around the tree in groups, they listen to the story of Savitri. After ending their fast, they give fruits, clothes and money in charity.

Preparations for the fast

On the day of Jyestha Krishna Trayodashi, after their morning ablutions, women usually apply a paste made of *gingli* (sesamum) and *amala* (Indian gooseberry) over their bodies and then take a bath. After this, they should eat the roots of the *vat vriksha* (banyan tree) along with water. The fast should be observed from Trayodashi to Purnima (full moon) or Amavasya for three nights. At dawn of the fourth day, one should break the fast by offering water to the moon.

At home, the women usually paint an image of the banyan tree using a paste made of turmeric and sandalwood. They then sit and offer prayers to it asking the goddess Savitri for her grace, so that one may accomplish this fast without facing any hurdles, with her blessings.

The popular belief is that in the roots of the banyan tree resides the Hindu Trinity of Gods. In its roots resides Brahma – the Creator, in the bark of the tree resides Vishnu – the Preserver, and in its top branches and foliage resides Shiva. The vat tree in its totality is representative of both the Goddess Savitri, and Savitri, the wife of Satyavan.

On the fourth day, women prepare delicious dishes and first offer these to the Goddess, then to the Brahmins, and after that to the rest of family.

Note:

There are no rigid rules regarding any Hindu fast. Working women, pregnant women, those who are menstruating, or suffering from some illness, and those who have just delivered a baby usually skip the fasting and just offer prayers to the Goddess.

Appendix 4

Kingdom of Madra

The Region of Madra

Madra, also called Madraka, was the name of an ancient region located near the city of Okara in present-day Pakistan. The Madras were an ancient kshatriya tribe of the Vedic times. *Aitareya Brahmana* makes the first reference to the Madras as Uttara Madras i.e. Northern Madras, the earliest settlement of the Madra clan, and locates them in the trans-Himalayan region as neighbours to the Uttara Kurus. The Uttara Madra country of Aitareya Brahmana is often identified with Bahlika (the Greek Bactria). The Southern Madras living to the south were an offshoot of the Uttara Madras.

Panini however documents the Madra republic as an Oligarchy (a State governed by a small group of fighting Kshatriya oligarchs like the Licchavi, Panchala, Malla, Kuru, Kekaya, to name a few) with its capital at Sakala or Sagala, corresponding to modern-day Sialkot in Pakistan. It appears that the Madras had cultural interactions with the region of Bahalika (Bactria) – also mentioned in some verses of the Mahabharata epic.

Origin of the Madras

An account preserved in the Puranas and the Mahabharata states that King Yayati, the great-grandson of King Pruravasa Aila, had five sons – Yadu, Turvasa, Anu, Druhyu and Puru. King Pruravasa Aila was, in turn, the grandson of Vaivasta

Manu, the mythological ancestor of all royal families of the Indian tradition. The Lunar line of kshatriya royal families are believed to have originated from this Pruravasa Aila. Puranic accounts indicate that the Madras were the direct descendants of Yayati's son Anu.

The Vamsa Brahmana of the Samaveda refers to Madragara Saungayani, an ancient Vedic teacher, from whom Aupamanyava, of the Kamboja tribe, received Vedic lore. This means that Vedic learning was widespread among the Madras and gave them a respected status among ancient teachers. This is also testified by the Satapatha Brahmana which mentions that sages of Northern India, most likely of the Kuru-Sanchala district, came to Madra to receive their Vedic education. For example, in the Brhadaranyaka Upanishad, Uddalaka Aruni tells Yajnavalkya, "We dwelt among the Madras in the houses of Patancala Kapya, studying the sacrifice."

The Kishkindha Kanda of Valmiki's Ramayana states that Sugriva, the brother who deposed King Bali of the Vanaras, with the help of Lord Rama and Hanuman, had sent his spies to search for Sita, wife of Lord Rama, in various lands of the Uttara patha including the Madras. While the Vishnu Purana mentions the Madras along with other tribes such as the Arama, Paraskia among others, the Matsya Purana mentions them along with Gandharas and Yavanas as well. A reference is also made in the Matsya Purana to King Aswapati of Sakala, father of Savitri, in the country of Madra.

The Mahabharata refers to a King Vyusitashva, a descendant of the famous King Puru of the Rigvedic era, of the Puru clan whose wife Bhadra bore seven sons – four of whom were Madras and three Salwas. This means that the Madras and Salwas belong to common stock.

Madri, the second wife of King Pandu of Hastinapur, and the mother of the Pandava brothers Nakul and Sahadev, was a Madra princess. The epic also refers to King Ashvapati or Aswapati of Madra who was the father of Savitri.

In the Adi Parva of Mahabharata, it is mentioned that King Shalya of Madra came with his two sons Rukmangada and Rukmaratha to the swayamvara of Draupadi.

King Shalya, who was the uncle of Nakula and Sahadeva of the Pandavas, came with his army to join them in the battle against the Kauravas to Upaplavya, the capital of the Matsya kingdom. However, he was intercepted on the way by Duryodhana and his men, who without revealing their identity, offered him and his troops lavish hospitality. Shalya was thus indebted to Duryodhana and had to ally with him during the battle. The last commander to lead the Kauravas into battle with the Pandavas, King Shalya was killed by Yudhishtra of the Pandavas on the last day of the battle at Kurukshetra.

The Arthashastra of Kautilya (4th century BCE) refers to the Madras as following a republican constitution and labels them as *Raja-shabd-opajivin* i.e. living by the title of Raja.

King Aswapati and Queen Malavi of Madra

Mahabharata, Book 3, Chapter 291: 'There was a king among the Madras, named Aswapati, who was virtuous and highly pious. And then by the grace of goddess Savitri, the embryo in the womb of Queen Malavi (wife of Aswapati) of the kingdom of Malava, increased like the lord of stars in the heavens during the lighted fortnight. And when the time came, she brought forth a daughter furnished with lotus-like eyes. She was the famous Savitri, who became wife of Prince Satyavan of the kingdom of Salwa.'

The kingdom of Madra continued till 9th century CE, when we find the Madras as allies of King Dharampala (770-810 CE) of the Pala Dynasty of Bengal, who with the connivance of the Madras and other northern powers, dethroned King Indraraja of Kanauj and placed Chakrayudha on the throne. According to some sources, Dharampala had seized the lands of Matsya, Madra, Kukru, Yadu, Avanti among some other northern kingdoms.

Madras of present-day

A gotra of North India claiming descent from the ancient Madras is found in various tribes/clans of the Med/Mair Rajputs in Rajasthan, Uttar Pradesh, Haryana, and Punjab. The Madrak, Madrayana or Maderna gotra Jats live in western Rajasthan. Those belonging to the Bhati gotra associate themselves with both Ghazni and Sialkot and for this reason the Bhati gotra Jats are accepted as a branch of the Madras. Among the Jat Sikhs, Madras are found in the Ambala district of Haryana, and near Rajpura in Fatehgarh district of Punjab.

The Vedic Age roughly corresponds to the Iron Age of civilisation.

Appendix 5

Kingdom of Salwa

Common Ancestry of Salwas and Madras

In ancient, pre-historic India, King Vyushitaswa of the Puru dynasty by performing the *ashwamedha* or horse-sacrifice yagna, established predominance over the neighbouring kingdoms of the North, East and West, exacting tributes from their kingdoms. Vyushitaswa had seven sons, three of whom became kings of Salwa and four became the kings of Madra.

(Mahabharata 1.121)

Location of Salwa Kingdom

The kingdom of Salwa, separated from Madra by the desolate desert kingdom of Matsya, lay south-west to the kingdom of Madra. A coastal kingdom to the north of the famous Dwarka along the Arabian Sea, it is reported to have had a strong naval fleet and a bustling trade with countries in the region which today comprises the Middle East. The capital city of Salwa was Saubha also known as Saubhaganagara.

King Dyumatsena of Salwa

Having gone blind, Dyumatsena was overthrown by a rival king of a neighbouring kingdom and sent into exile along with his wife Saivya and the infant Satyavan. They sought refuge in the hermitage of Rishi Dalbhaya in the forests of Salwa. Satyavan, during his childhood, is also sometimes referred to as

Chitraswa or Chitrasen because as a young lad, he was fond of drawing horses as well as making horses out of clay.

(Mahabharata 3.292)

Salwa kings in the time of Mahabharata War

A prince of Salwa is mentioned as being present in the swayamvara of Princess Panchali (Draupadi) in the court of her father, King Drupad of Panchala.

Jayadratha, king of Sindhu-Sauvira, married to Princess Dussala and thereby brother-in-law to Duryodhana of the Kauravas, is said to have travelled through the Kamyaka woods to the kingdom of Salwa whose King Saubha was a close friend and ally.

(Mahabharata 3.262)

King Saubha also launched an attack on Dwarka in which he was said to have been killed by Krishna. The narrative credits him with having an aircraft known as Saubha Vimana, which he used for travel and aerial warfare.

Bibliography

Mahabharata of Krishna Dwaipayana Vyasa, Book 3: Vana Parva – Pativrata-mahatmya Parva (Section CCLXLI – CCLXLVII), English translation by K. M. Ganguli

Savitri – A Legend and a Symbol, Sri Aurobindo

Savitri and Satyavan: The Path to Immortality, Vladimir Yatsenko

Savitri: The Legend and departures made by Sri Aurobindo, R. Y. Deshpande

Yama – Encyclopaedia Brittanica

The Culture and Civilisation of Ancient India, D. D. Kosambi

Some Ksatriya Tribes of Ancient India – Dr. Bimla Charan Law, P.hD, Fellow of Royal Historical Society, London

Early History of India, V.A. Smith

Consciousness Studies, Shankara Bharadwaj Khandavalli

Savitri – Wikipedia – the free encyclopedia

Savitr – Wikipedia – the free encyclopedia

Salwa Kingdom – Wikipedia – the free encyclopedia

The Story of Savitri and Satyavan, H. A. Guerber

Hindus: Their Religious Beliefs and Practices, Julius Lipner

Dharma: Its Early History in Law, Religion and Narrative – contributed by Alf Hiltebeitel

Savitri Brata Katha, Translated from Oriya into English by Oriya Nari Team

Aswapati's Yoga-Tapasya: He became vast by his largeness, The Light of the Supreme (blogs/light-of-supreme/posts)

About the Author

An alumunus of St. Stephen's college, Shivdutt Sharma graduated with Honours in History and did his post-graduation in English Literature. Working as a senior Copywriter and subsequently as a Creative Director with several advertising agencies in Mumbai, he is now an Editor with a publishing firm. His earlier published works include books for children that impart moral values, and a personal memoir titled 'The Hill Billy' – of his early years in Mussoorie. He presently resides in Mumbai.

The author may be contacted on email:
shivds@gmail.com

For further details, contact:
Yogi Impressions LLP
1711, Centre 1, World Trade Centre,
Cuffe Parade, Mumbai 400 005, India.

Fill in the Mailing List form on our website and receive, via email, information on books, authors, events and more.
Visit: www.yogiimpressions.com

Telephone: (022) 61541500, 61541541
E-mail: yogi@yogiimpressions.com

TITLES BY SHIVDUTT SHARMA AVAILABLE FROM YOGI IMPRESSIONS

Mythology / Romance

Autobiography / Memoir

Children's Books

Available as E-book

Available as E-book

Available as E-book